Cool Spaces!

Cool Spaces!
The Best New Architecture

Art Spaces, Libraries, Performance Spaces, Healing Spaces

Based on the TV show hosted by
STEPHEN CHUNG

ORO
EDITIONS

Contents

Introduction

by Stephen Chung, AIA
Host, Cool Spaces!

In the popular sitcom Seinfeld, one of the main characters, George Costanza, compulsively lies to impress the people he meets. One of his favorite claims is telling people that he is an architect. George loves the idea of being an architect. Never mind that George doesn't have any interest in the subject or even really understands what an architect does, all he knows is that the mere mention of being an architect gives him a sense of false pride that makes him giddy. When asked by Jerry's inquisitive girlfriend what kinds of buildings he designs, he fumbles and blurts out that he "designs railroads" and that "it's really not that hard." Of course, railroad design is more closely associated with civil engineering, not architecture. And yes, being an architect is hard. But no matter, George enjoys telling people that he is an architect even more than exaggerating athletic accomplishments or romantic partners. Why? What's so great about being an architect?

When I was a kid, I always wanted to be an architect. The idea of making a drawing and then building at full scale seemed like the coolest thing. Like a lot of kids, I played with Legos and made all kinds of forts. But very much unlike the others, I started signing my homework as "Stephen Chung and Associates," written in the same lettering style that I saw on building blueprints. Of course, seeing "Associates" on my homework aroused the suspicion in my teachers. I explained it was going to be the name of my future architecture office—not a covert admission that my homework was a collaborative effort.

With a single-minded focus, I took mechanical drafting and art classes as part of my high school class load, and went to special summer programs in architecture for high school students, before heading off to college to begin my career in architecture as an undergraduate. After five grueling years, I kept at it without any break and went straight into another two years to pursue my master's degree in architecture. After seven long years of intensive study, I began working as a young architect and slaved away as a poorly paid intern. Despite the long road, I wasn't discouraged at all. On the contrary, I felt like it was a well-traveled path, and I was convinced that this was the way to become a great architect. The next fifteen years took me through a wide array of experiences as both a practicing architect and teacher. During this time, I was so fully submersed in my work that I didn't really see architecture in context. It wasn't until the housing crash in 2007-08 that I was able to step back and assess where I was. Actually, I didn't have much choice. With so few commissions available at the time to me, there was much time to think.

A short time after the crash, I began to research the state of the architecture profession for a white paper. What emerged from that study was a focus on a designer who had successfully found a way to flourish, even in difficult economic times: Phillipe Starck. I had the opportunity to work with Philippe firsthand on a project in Boston a couple years earlier and came away impressed by his ability to communicate his message to the general public. His work connected with people—and not just the design community. Inspired by his example, I sought out a way to "bridge the gap" between the profession and general public in my own way. I abandoned the white paper idea and tried to think of another way where I could reach more people and make more of a difference. In essence, I wanted to find a way to share my passion

for architecture with the general public in hopes that it would better explain what architects do and why it's important. I figured that if I could increase general interest in architecture, there would be more opportunities for architects to build. With the combination of more opportunities afforded for architects with a more engaged general public, the quality of the built environment would be greatly improved. And by that I mean: it could be better built, less costly, more sustainable, more beautiful, and so on. Everyone would benefit. Too ambitious, you say? I think this is a quality that afflicts many architects.

For me, "bridging the gap" has taken the form of a television show. To this end, I am the host of a series on public television entitled *Cool Spaces! The Best New Architecture*. For the inaugural season, we are presenting four hour-long episodes, with each show revolving around a common function such as art or healing spaces. For each theme, we profile three very different buildings, designed by very different architects in very different cities. Taken together, each episode highlights a tremendous range of creative and artful problem-solving. As part of the show concept, we made two key decisions: 1) that the buildings had to be public, meaning that they would be places people could actually visit for themselves; and 2) that the buildings had to contemporary, or as we defined it, be built within ten years. With this parameter, we figured that most people wouldn't have yet visited the selected buildings—not all of them, anyway.

When it came to the selection of the particular buildings, I wish I could say that there was some complex algorithm that made the decisions for us. In reality, it was the result of a team of three people— Dan Frank, the producer, and John Hawkes, the director of photography, and me—sifting through a huge pile of contemporary public buildings. Yes, I would propose many (to my mind exciting) possibilities, but unless the building met a wide range of criteria, it would get rejected. Dan would be looking for interesting characters and a great storyline, while John would be thinking about the views and the potential for different "looks." Finally, after a lot of debate, we arrived at twelve contemporary buildings—exemplary architecture designed by some of the top architects in the world. In each case, the architect is presented with a difficult design challenge and impossibly high expectations. Do they succeed? Well, if you haven't seen the show yet, I'll let you in on something: in our version of the world, the architect always comes out as the hero. Yes, George Costanza, I can see why you would want to pretend be an architect.

www.coolspaces.tv

Art Spaces

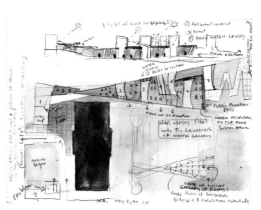

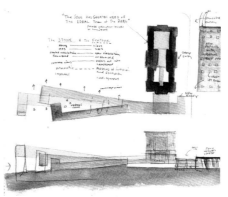

[FAR LEFT] Sketch showing the new building along the side of the existing building.

[LEFT] Sketch highlighting the contrast between existing building and new.

[RIGHT] Model showing Steven's ingenious concept to place the building off to the side of the original museum building.

Bloch Building
at the Nelson-Atkins Museum of Art

by Steven Holl Architects
Kansas City, Missouri

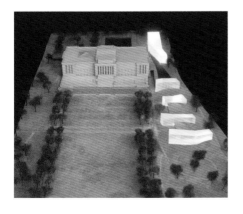

The story of the Bloch Building at the Nelson-Atkins Museum of Art demonstrates the typical elements of an architecture project. From the initial need of the client to the architect's design solution, the project also illustrates how a strong concept and shared mission successfully bring a building to life.

The Nelson-Atkins Museum of Art is a world-renowned institution that is free to the public. As the museum entered the 21st century, the museum board wanted to expand Nelson-Atkins' physical and functional capacities. The expansion would allow the museum to provide better support spaces, acquire and display more art, and offer more educational programs.

The original 1933 building, designed by Kansas City firm Wight and Wight, displays the striking symmetry and ornamentation that define the Beaux-Arts style of architecture. The museum is also an icon to the citizens of Kansas City. So the museum required an expansion that would respect the community's attachment to the existing building.

When museum leaders started the process of choosing an architect, they took an academic approach. After culling six firms from a list of hundreds, the selection committee presented each firm with a sketchbook meant to be filled over the course of two months. Instead of fully formed building models, the committee wanted to see two-dimensional ideas that illustrated the architects' design process and understanding of the project.

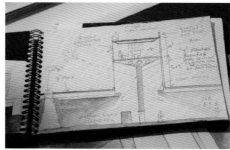

[FAR LEFT] Looking at key watercolor sketches for building.
[LEFT AND BELOW LEFT] Holl is known for his unique creative process, which begins with free-flowing watercolor sketches. Nearly all of the major design ideas begin here.

[OPPOSITE, TOP] New and old harmoniously living together.
[OPPOSITE, BOTTOM LEFT] Grassy paths between the translucent structures provide places for visitors to walk around and over the galleries.
[OPPOSITE, BOTTOM RIGHT] Part of the addition involved designing a new shallow pool of water in entry court.

[BELOW] The Bloch's lantern-like buildings step down the Nelson-Atkins site.

The museum board implied a preference for a site north of the existing building by requiring that designs preserve the great lawn and the view of the building's south facade. Placing the new structure against the north facade and blocking that view of the Wight and Wight design seemed like the only real solution, and five of the architecture firms proposed just that. One, however, had a different idea.

The design by Steven Holl Architects broke the unwritten rule of the committee and eclipsed everyone's expectations.

Holl was inspired by a painting he had seen in the museum's collection: a Chinese scroll depicting a scholar's home partly visible through rocks and trees and nestled into the hillside. The image of a place of reflection, a close relationship to the landscape, and the partially hidden views in and out guided Holl's concept.

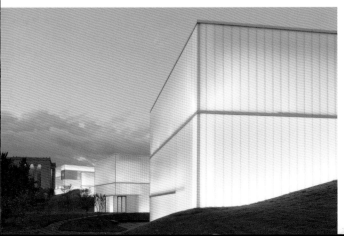

[LEFT] View of the Bloch Building sitting below the original museum.
[ABOVE] The translucent structures are inviting and intriguing.

[BELOW LEFT] Sketch of sculpture court dedicated to the works of Isamu Noguchi.

[BELOW] Discussing the Isamu Noguchi sculpture court. The court provides visitors a place to reflect and view the surrounding Kansas City Sculpture Park.

[ABOVE] Stephen speaks with Henry Bloch, the founder of H&R Block, for whom the building is named.

Holl's sketches described a series of glowing boxes that hugged the landscape next to the original building. Immediately rejecting the idea of an appendage, he planned a separate structure on the eastern side of the original museum, not the north. Instead of hiding the new building behind the original, Holl wanted to sink most of the new structure underground. Periodically, the addition's transluscent lightboxes would pop up and form the roofs of the new galleries.

The selection committee unanimously chose Holl for his sensitive design, which respected the original building but still projected a modern identity. By breaking the large addition into into smaller pieces, Holl's design gently deferred to the original Nelson-Atkins and enhanced the existing landscape design.

The Bloch Building, named for H&R Block founder Henry W. Bloch and his wife, Marion, features five translucent boxes that direct light into galleries below. At night, these lightboxes glow like lanterns. The lightboxes also serve as additional pieces of the Nelson-Atkins' sculpture gardens. Grass paths grow between the boxes, inviting visitors to walk around and over to explore the entire museum grounds. Since the Nelson-Atkins is free to the public at all times, Holl was able to create a very open, accessible design.

[FAR LEFT] Dynamic ramps and stairs draw visitors through the galleries.
[LEFT] Stephen with project architect Greg Sheldon of BNIM.
[BELOW] Echoing the lightboxes, lenses in the plaza and reflecting pool shine light down into the garage.
[OPPOSITE] Natural light accentuates angled interior walls.

Inside the lightboxes, Holl created sculptural ceilings that direct light along curves, so that walls appear washed in light. To address the damaging effects of light on art, Holl varied the height of the galleries. As each gallery level gradually steps down in response to the slope of the landscape, the ceilings step higher. The gallery walls curve to direct natural light into the spaces but away from the artwork.

Although the Bloch Building projects a strong image, the architecture does not compete or distract from the artwork inside the galleries. The forms are simple, and the lighting is even and calming so that visitors can quietly enjoy the art.

Using light as if it were a material is a trademark skill of Steven Holl, and even the garage of the Bloch Building benefits from natural light.

A large art installation by artist Walter De Maria sits above the parking garage in the plaza formed by the Bloch Building and the original museum building. The piece is formed by a reflecting pool and clear lenses. As with the lightboxes, the lenses direct daylight into the parking garage below. At night, aboveground, the lenses glow with the light from inside the parking garage.

The design of the Bloch Building at the Nelson-Atkins Museum of Art demonstrates that an addition can complement an existing building while simultaneously projecting a powerful identity.

The Barnes Foundation

by Tod Williams Billie Tsien Architects
Philadelphia, Pennsylvania

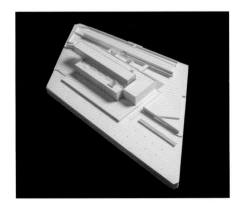

One of the newest additions to Philadelphia's Benjamin Franklin Parkway, the city's boulevard of civic and cultural institutions, is a suburban transplant. The Barnes Foundation museum originally housed the personal art collections of Dr. Albert C. Barnes in the quiet residential suburb of Merion. Dr. Barnes, an American chemist and businessman of the early 20th century, built his impressive gallery away from the city to make his masterworks by Renoir, Cezanne, Picasso, and Matisse available to the working class.

Barnes arranged his art in a very personal salon style, tightly grouping the artworks with objects he felt reinforced the impact of the paintings. He called the grouped arrangements "ensembles." To protect his collection, Barnes established a trust: the Barnes Foundation. His will outlined his wishes for maintaining every single piece in the precise position he had placed it.

Although the Barnes Gallery presented a very unique and highly personal museum experience, visiting the gallery in such a remote location was difficult. The residential neighborhood restricted parking and hours and limited the number of visitors the gallery could accommodate. In addition, seeing the work in a house setting was not optimal as far as lighting and other environmental factors, such as air quality.

Following Dr. Barnes' death in 1951, the foundation board worked on making the collections available to more people while still respecting Dr. Barnes' will. The board members felt that moving the collections from a residential suburban setting to the city would make the collections more accessible to a larger population. In 2004, after extended legal proceedings, a court ruled that the collections could be moved but that the ensembles and the sequence of rooms in the original gallery had to be preserved.

[LEFT] Study model showing the basic composition of two bars and a floating glass box.

[RIGHT] The lightbox extends past the main wings of the building forms a dramatic canopy.

[FAR RIGHT] Original Barnes Foundation gallery building in Merion, Pennsylvania.

[LEFT] Stephen with Billie Tsien and Tod Williams in their NYC studio. Here, Tod explains a design concept using a wood study model.

[BELOW] Block model used by the architects in their interviews to demonstrate their concept of inserting gardens into the galleries.

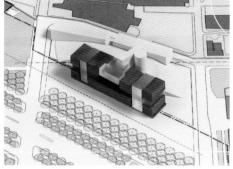

[RIGHT] Stephen introduces the Barnes Foundation segment with Tod and Billie on one of the public plazas surrounding the museum.

The search for an architect to design the new Barnes Foundation included every major architect in the world. During the selection interviews, most of the architects presented design proposals. Ultimately, the architects who did not immediately offer a design solution were selected. Tod Williams Billie Tsien Architects reasoned that the project had to be a collaboration from the start, between foundation and architecture firm, in order to be successful. The husband-and-wife design team's inclusive approach and thoughtful exploration of concepts won the committee over.

Williams and Tsien faced strict design guidelines for the new building, most notably in the galleries. After visiting and studying the original Barnes Foundation, the architects realized that the experience of the original gallery rooms could only be replicated by reproducing the original scale, proportion, and configuration of spaces.

Once the design limitations on the gallery spaces were accepted, the architects were free to concentrate on designing a new building on a new site. The firm improved the museum experience with controlled lighting, expressive materials, and a gracious relationship to the museum's civic neighbors.

[ABOVE] Visitors enter over a reflecting pool to the main entrance.

The original Merion gallery was built in the middle of an arboretum established by Dr. Barnes' wife, Laura. To reach the building, visitors walked through landscaped gardens. The landscaped entry sequence inspired Williams and Tsien's concept of creating "a gallery within a garden, and a garden within a gallery."

The new Barnes Foundation building is surrounded by a series of gardens. The landscaped areas create public spaces that connect the new building to its urban surroundings. Sitting areas modeled after porches open onto landscaped terraces and provide access to garden levels that step down the site's gentle slope. The architects placed another garden between the gallery rooms, to give visitors a breather from the incredibly dense arrangement of artwork.

Williams and Tsien studied the original floor plans to decipher where improvements could be made without compromising the original sequence. They found that a central structural wall split the building in half. The architects took the opportunity to create a new in-between space. In the new gallery, visitors walk around a glass-enclosed, open-air garden instead of a thick solid wall.

[LEFT] One of the porch spaces that open onto landscaped gardens.

[ABOVE] View of the gallery garden from the lobby.

[RIGHT] Sketch by Billie Tsien diagramming the basic concept of a gallery within a garden and a garden within a gallery.

[FAR RIGHT] "Garden in the gallery" concept realized.

gallery in a garden

garden in a gallery

[ABOVE] View of the grand foyer space. Natural light pours in from above through a carefully shaped skylight.

[LEFT] Stephen with Billie and Tod in the great room.

[OPPOSITE, TOP LEFT] Sketch illustrating the lighting scheme that brings diffuse natural light into the gallery spaces through clerestory windows.

[OPPOSITE, TOP RIGHT] Sketch of the sculptural ceilings within the lightbox.

[OPPOSITE, BOTTOM] Throughout the museum, the designers introduced domestic touches such as smaller scale furniture groupings and a herringbone pattern of the floor for a residential feel.

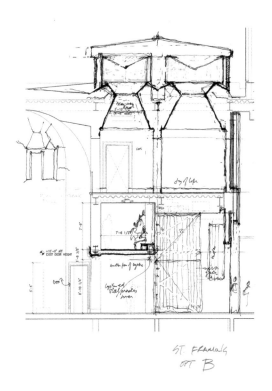

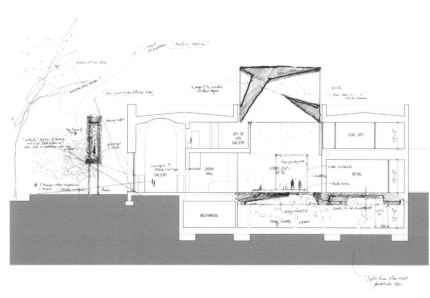

ST. FRAMING
OPT B

The original gallery faced south, and windows were always covered with curtains to protect against the damaging effects of light. The heavy drapes, however, also obscured the colors of the art and made viewing the pieces difficult. In the new Barnes, Williams and Tsien used the same south-facing orientation but designed a new natural lighting scheme. The design team placed high windows, or clerestories, on a second level to create diffuse light for the gallery spaces without directly casting light on the art.

A long interior court separates the gallery wing from the wing containing public functions including the lobby, library, auditorium, café, and meeting rooms. Above the court, a large lightbox sits over the space with a sculpted ceiling. The folded planes of the ceiling allow indirect light into the court, inspiring the name: light court. On the exterior, the roof of the light court dramatically projects beyond the main wings of the building and establishes a bright, halo-like presence along Benjamin Franklin Parkway.

The architects also maintained a connection to the original building through a sensitive selection of materials. African motifs surrounding the entrance of the original Barnes gallery inspired the architects to think of the building skin like a stone cloth. For the new Barnes Foundation, Williams and Tsien clad the exterior in a pattern of large stone panels that mimics patterns found in Kente cloth. The warm tones in the stones emphasize the richness and variety that can be found in the material.

By working with the constraints of the project, Tod Williams Billie Tsien Architects designed a modern building that fit into its new urban context while still paying homage to the original gallery.

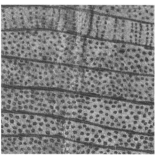

[FAR LEFT] Sketch of the Jacobs Ladder concept layered on the African textile patterns.
[LEFT] Inspiration image of African textile.
[RIGHT] Stephen with David Taylor, director of the Harvey B. Gantt Center for African-American Arts + Culture.

Harvey B. Gantt Center
for African-American Arts + Culture

by Freelon Group
Charlotte, North Carolina

The Harvey B. Gantt Center is a community center for African and African-American arts, culture, and community outreach. The center was named in honor of Harvey Bernard Gantt, a well-respected community leader, businessman, and Charlotte's first African-American mayor. Gantt is also an architect who competed for the museum project. Although his firm did not win the commission, having the building named after him was a pretty good consolation prize. The architects who were ultimately chosen, Freelon Group, helped the institution find a home in what was once the center of Charlotte's black community.

The Brooklyn neighborhood was a thriving African-American community in Charlotte during the era of separate but equal laws. The stand-alone downtown district encompassed hospitals, schools, churches, and businesses. Following desegregation and urban renewal efforts in the 1960s, Brooklyn and other neighborhoods were slowly torn down to make way for an expanding central business district.

After witnessing the displacement of historic black neighborhoods, Charlotte's black community leaders began efforts to preserve and celebrate the contributions of African-Americans, and those of African descent, to American culture. The leaders formed an organization originally named Afro-American Cultural Center and based the headquarters in the old Little Rock AME Zion Church. As the center grew, the leaders realized the need for a dedicated building to be able to provide more programs for the community and to bring national attention to their mission.

[ABOVE LEFT] With Harvey B. Gantt, the first black mayor of Charlotte, whom the center was named after. [ABOVE RIGHT] Stephen with Freelon Group architects in the firm's office.

[BELOW, TOP TO BOTTOM]
Sketch of the Jacobs
Ladder concept layered
on the African textile
patterns.
[RIGHT] Former building
that housed the Afro-
American Cultural Center.

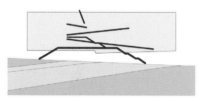

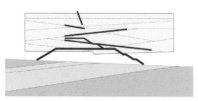

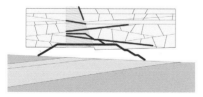

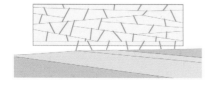

When Freelon Group was selected to design the new center, the site under consideration was a narrow strip of land in the growing cultural district of Charlotte that was once part of the historic Brooklyn neighborhood. The extremely long site was, in fact, a ramp to the parking garage of an adjacent development. The clients were understandably concerned that this "leftover" site would not be manageable and wanted to find an alternative site in another part of town. Freelon Group felt strongly that the new building had to be in the cultural district. They asked the client for a week to study the site and to see if they could come up was a creative solution. Once the client was convinced the site was workable, Freelon Group began its design process.

In such a culturally rich area, the designers researched historic photos, the urban context, and African heritage to form an architectural solution. One of the landmark buildings the designers studied was the Myer School, an anchor of Charlotte's African-American community in the mid-20th century. The school had a prominent fire escape stair that inspired the nickname of "Jacob's Ladder School." For the Brooklyn community, the stairs were a symbol of hope and the power of education to uplift. This historic reference is a guiding concept for the Gantt Center.

The challenges of the complicated site helped the architects work out how to integrate the form of the stairs into the new building. To maintain access to the garage entrance, the architects decided to lift the new building so that the main lobby would be on the second floor. The system of ramps, escalators, and stairs to enter the Gantt Center is a modern interpretation of the Jacob's Ladder.

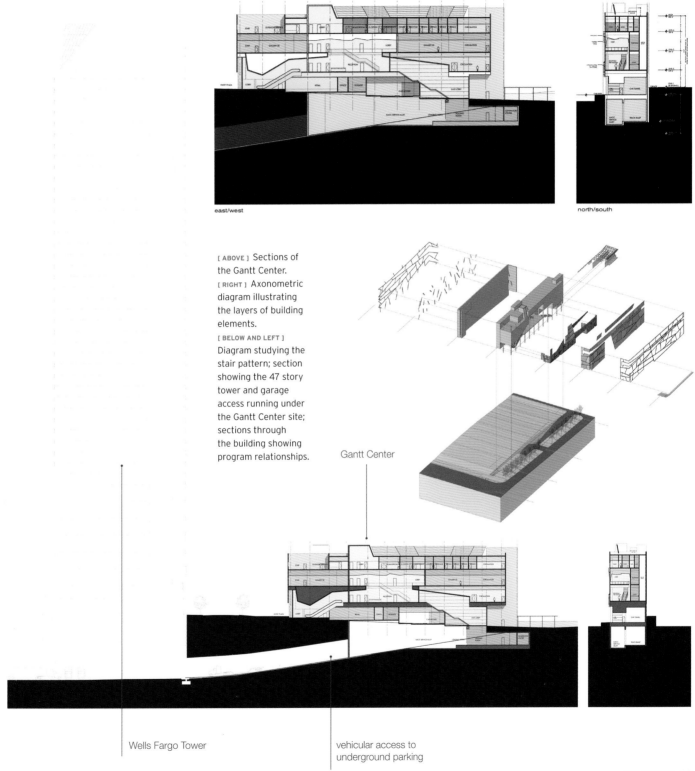

east/west

north/south

[ABOVE] Sections of
the Gantt Center.
[RIGHT] Axonometric
diagram illustrating
the layers of building
elements.
[BELOW AND LEFT]
Diagram studying the
stair pattern; section
showing the 47 story
tower and garage
access running under
the Gantt Center site;
sections through
the building showing
program relationships.

Gantt Center

Wells Fargo Tower

vehicular access to
underground parking

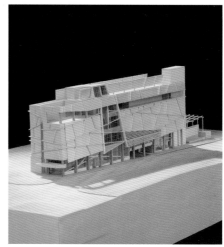

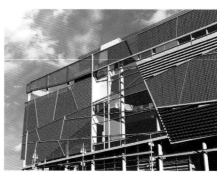

[TOP LEFT] View of the
rear elevation at night.
[TOP RIGHT] Model of
the Gantt Center.
[LEFT] Exterior view of
the glass enclosed atrium.
[ABOVE] Rendering of
the final metal panel
and glass main facade.

[BELOW] Diagram of
the rear elevation light
sculpture

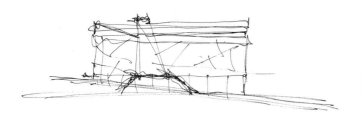

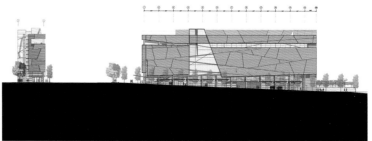

[ABOVE LEFT AND MIDDLE] Early facade renderings studying glass and metal panel relationships.
[ABOVE] Massing model of the Gantt Center showing solid and glass relationships.

Since the location also faced an entry point into the downtown area, the architects realized the building's facade would serve as a very prominent billboard. The exterior skin would be critical to communicating the center's purpose.

To attract attention and represent the institution's mission, Freelon Group designed a bold pattern based on woven textiles from West Africa and quilt designs from the Underground Railroad. The materials of the main facade are perforated metal panels that appear stitched together with diagonal steel channels. The jagged lines running across a very rectilinear building create a compelling image that reflects the excitement and energy within the building.

The architects continued the textile inspired pattern on the north side of the building, which faced a site slated for future development. In place of metal panels and aluminum strips, the north facade is simple stucco accented with strip lighting. This side of the building was treated like a light sculpture to break up what could be an unfriendly public face. Although the north may eventually be hidden behind a future development, the quilting pattern is repeated on this side. The windowless face also provided a logical place to organize some of the galleries, since they do not need outward views.

[FAR LEFT] Phil Freelon reviews plans with a staff member.
[LEFT] Artist Chris Johnson discusses his Gantt Center exhibition.

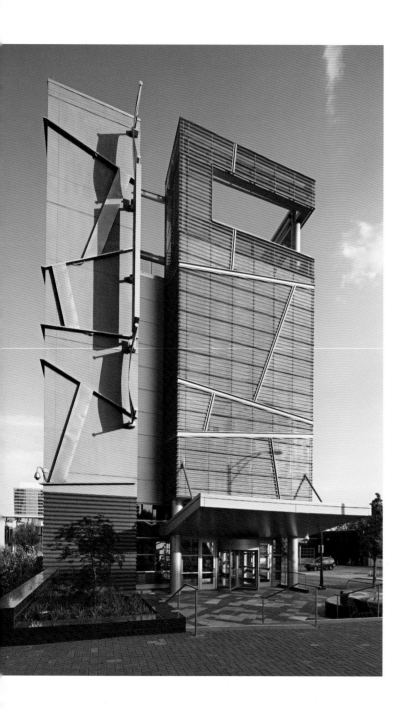

Inside the building, stairs and escalators frame a dramatic four-story central atrium to repeat the Jacob's Ladder concept. The architects translated the exterior quilt motif into a sculptural, folded drywall ceiling in the lobby. The galleries were designed to keep the spotlight on the art, with dark carpets and ceilings. For the center's staff, the classroom space was very important, since the classroom most reflects the center's origins and mission. The new state-of-the-art space accommodates workshops, seminars, training programs, and lectures to support the institution's outreach role. At the building's top, a roof deck provides wonderful views of Charlotte and allows those who have lived through the city's transformation to reflect on how far the city has come.

The Harvey B. Gantt Center for African-American Arts + Culture commemorates the history of Charlotte's black community by reclaiming the historically significant location. The striking building brings the institution onto the national stage of defining and celebrating African and African-American arts and culture.

The Case for Cool Spaces

by Robert Ivy, FAIA
EVP/Chief Executive Officer, The American Institute of Architects

Architecture, the ancient and constantly renewing discipline, forms the foundation of our everyday lives. It shapes our world in visible ways by defining the streetscape and the skyline. It also shapes our world in tangible ways by creating spaces where we live, work, and play in relative safety and comfort.

The real power, however, resides in the intangible. That's where that multi-dimensional mystery and power reside. There's no other way I can express the feeling of experiencing the resonance of Los Angeles' Disney Concert Hall, sheltering a cellist in its warm vastness, or walking from shadowed 63rd Street into the light of New York's Central Park.

Architect Stephen Chung, AIA, calls such spaces cool. He's right. Cool spaces such as these are the subjects of this book, which draws together twelve recent architectural works that affect the lives of ordinary people like you and me in extraordinary ways.

"Cool spaces" is also the subject of a public television series conceived, assembled, and hosted by Stephen—the first major exploration and discussion about architecture in the national media in decades. Highly approachable, using everyday language, our host draws us into interesting projects, unlocking architecture for a generation that values design but wants to learn more. He asks obvious questions that most of us would like to ask: Who wanted this done? Why? What did they hope to accomplish? Why do these buildings look and feel the way they do? And, ultimately, what did it take to bring them to fruition? Over the course of a single episode, he demystifies architecture by making it understandable and approachable, allowing us to love and learn simultaneously.

In order to attract us, he picked a winner's list of architects and projects, from the most famous architect in the world to a hip, youngish shop that is pushing the boundaries of place-making: New York's SHoP Architects, Snøhetta, Steven Holl Architects, and Tod Williams Billie Tsien Architects; Boston's Safdie Architects; Durham's Freelon Group; Atlanta's Mack Scogin Merrill Elam Architects; HKS, which has offices on five continents; Phoenix's Richärd+Bauer; LMN, from Seattle; Rotterdam's OMA; and CO Architects and Gehry Partners, in Los Angeles.

We at the AIA are proud to underwrite **Cool Spaces!** and to have encouraged our member, the talented Stephen, to share his appreciation with you. From individual structures to neighborhoods to cities, he shows how architects employ their unique, visionary discipline—involving social, analytical, and technological skills—to make a better world.

It's hardly a stretch to say that architecture comprises every major building on every major street in every major city (and small ones, too). These few examples stand in for a world of buildings. You and I can walk through New York, San Francisco, London, or our own hometowns with newly opened eyes, thanks to **Cool Spaces!**

Use your new insight and enjoy.

Robert Ivy is the CEO of the American Institute of Architects and a former editor-in-chief of Architectural Record. He has been recognized for lifetime contributions to business media and for communicating the value of design to a new generation. Robert received his Bachelor of Arts from the University of the South, in Tennessee, and his Master in Architecture from Tulane University, Louisiana.

Libraries

Seattle Central Library

by OMA/REX with LMN
Seattle, Washington

[TOP] Stephen Chung with Deborah Jacobs, city librarian during the design and construction of the library. Jacobs was instrumental in getting the building realized.
[BOTTOM] Rem Koolhaas, principal of OMA. The design team held many presentations with the community to shape the library.

When architect OMA (Office for Metropolitan Architecture) was chosen to design a new central branch for the Seattle Public Library, the designers understood that libraries, and the role they play, were changing. Their new project required not only designing a modern library building, but also interpreting what a modern library would contain. To tackle the difficult task of redefining libraries for the 21st century, the architects embarked on a three-month long research journey and took their clients, and the city librarians, along for the ride.

The team's extensive research gathered information from librarians, technology and business gurus like Bill Gates, students and professors from Ivy League universities, and even the U.S. Department of Justice. The research also included field trips to libraries across the United States and Europe. The architects' and librarians' immersive learning experience helped the designers and their clients understand each other so that the team could shape the modern public library together.

City Librarian Deborah Jacobs in particular helped the architects understand the library's needs. Jacobs' desire for a library that brought people together guided the team's vision.

One of the most important lessons the team learned was that even in digital times, the book would not be going away. It would, however, have to share space with other forms of information like music, video, and the internet. Similarly, libraries as organizations and buildings would be sticking around, and they also would have to make room for other functions, especially providing internet access and spaces for the public. The team realized that libraries would return to their historical role as important civic buildings where people gathered and shared knowledge.

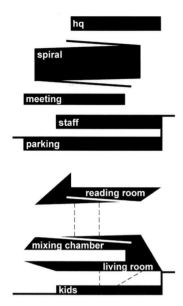

[ABOVE] Stacking diagram (top) of the Library's main functional groups. Stacking diagrams are used by architects to show vertical relationships between spaces and functions within a building. Stacking diagram (bottom) of the in-between interaction spaces.
[RIGHT] Stephen interviews window washers as they clean the glass facades of the building.

The architects spent a significant amount of time understanding the functions and relationships within a library. Using the basic organizing method of placing like objects with like objects in designated boxes, the architects established that there were five major groups of functional areas:

1. Administrative offices
2. Book stacks
3. Staff production areas
4. Meeting areas
5. Parking garage

The design of the building developed from a diagrammatic study of stacking, staggering, and then pulling apart the five boxes. Pulling apart the boxes created overlapping spaces. The architects used these in-between spaces for places where visitors could interact with librarians, information, and each other. The diagram of interaction areas sandwiched between major function areas became the shape of the building.

Once the puzzle of organizing the many functions was solved, the architects concentrated on creating a building that was transparent and open, important qualities for a space meant for the public. Using glass was the obvious choice, and OMA and Seattle architects LMN worked with engineers to design a custom glass-and-steel facade, or curtain wall, with glass panels set in a diamond-shaped grid. The curtain wall was applied like a glass net that effectively shrink-wrapped the building, following the ins and outs of the floors. The overall effect is a monumental jewel box that showcases the activity inside the library.

[ABOVE] Study model of the building design. The shape of the Seattle Central Library is a literal representation of the functions of the building.
[RIGHT] Stephen with Sam Miller of LMN, the local Seattle architecture firm that worked with OMA.

[LEFT] View of a sloping column next to the canted steel and glass walls.

[TOP] View of the
main lobby, or as
the architects call
it, the Living Room.
[FAR LEFT] An overhead
view of book stacks in
the main lobby.
[LEFT] View through
the mesh curtain over
glass wall.

[LEFT] View of the yellow escalators that surround the Book Spiral.
[RIGHT] The ingenious steel grid of the Library is both a seismic system and curtain wall, holding glass panels and transferring seismic loads to the concrete base of the building.

[BELOW] Joshua Prince-Ramus of REX and former OMA architect who spearheaded the project.

Since sunlight is harmful to books, the architects chose insulating glass panels with an embedded metal mesh to deflect the sun's rays as well as heat and glare. The mesh is made from expanded aluminum sheet metal that is cut and stretched to produce openings that act as a system of tiny louvers. From a distance and certain angles, the mesh would barely be visible to patrons. The mesh also made the glass very expensive.

Because the library was a publicly funded project, the budget could not afford the added cost of a premium glass. The mesh-embedded glass was reduced to only those surfaces that would receive direct sunlight, but the cost still exceeded the budget. The designers so believed in the energy and aesthetic advantages of using the mesh-embedded glass that they went on a fundraising mission themselves. Over a short span of ten days, the architects of OMA and LMN plead their case with Seattle's wealthy and philanthropic citizens and raised $3.2 million to cover the additional cost.

The dramatic sloping walls of the glass curtain wall are clearly visible from anywhere in the building, and the architects made every effort to keep the space as open as possible. After all of the effort spent on developing the skin of the building, the last thing the architects and their clients wanted to see was a dense grid of columns and beams.

Working closely together, the architecture and engineering teams developed a system of columns that could slope and transfer vertical loads down from level to level. Exposing and expressing structural elements is a hallmark of OMA's work and in the Seattle Central Library, the architects color-coded the structural elements so the system can be understood easily. Elements that support vertical loads—such as

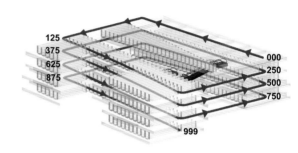

[ABOVE] The "pillowy" fabric contrasts with the sharp, angled steel and glass window walls.

[RIGHT] Diagram of the Book Spiral which allows the Library's main collections to be held in one continuous, ramping space.

columns, beams, and walls are grey, while the glass-and-aluminum curtain wall, which resists lateral or seismic forces, is light blue.

The architects used color coding throughout the building to help orient and direct visitors. The mixing chamber, which is the library's full-service information center, is a high-tech scheme of black and silver. Bright, lipstick-red staircases and hallways are used to draw attention and lead to the public meeting rooms. Glowing chartreuse staircases and escalators identify the circulation. The vivid staircases also lead to another important product of the design team's research: the Book Spiral.

The Book Spiral is the designated area for the library's main collection of books. The team observed that although the Dewey Decimal System is a continuous numbering system, in most libraries the collections were divided into different rooms, breaking up the natural sequence. For the Seattle Central Library, the architects developed a spiral organizing system with terraced shelving and browsing areas that could hold the entire collection in one continuously ramping, four-story space. The single space allows visitors to easily navigate through topics without jumping rooms or numbers. The system also accommodates the expansion and contraction of the collection.

Like any successful design solution, the Seattle Central Library developed from intensive user research, a clear understanding of program, and a great relationship between client and design team. With a straightforward design approach, OMA/REX and LMN created a stunning monument that provides a welcoming experience for visitors, an efficient place to work for librarians, and a truly public building for the citizens of Seattle.

James B. Hunt Jr. Library

by Snøhetta with Clark Nexsen
Raleigh, North Carolina

In 2008, North Carolina State University decided its campus needed a new library. The university's existing library buildings were too small for the number of students and too outdated to represent the school's mission to be a gateway of the world's knowledge.

The university saw an opportunity to take what traditionally holds the brains of a university campus and infuse it with a social heart and intellectual soul. They wanted a modern building that would foster collaboration and learning.

Awarding a large project typically involves a long process of interviewing design teams and sifting through large packages of materials that include resumes, past projects, recommendations, and a schematic design proposal. North Carolina State University, however, wanted to ensure that it found the ideal team to design a signature library. Instead of the usual rounds of formal presentations, the university reviewed hundreds of submissions and short-listed six teams to participate in a three-day design workshop on its campus.

After the design workshop, Norwegian and New York-based firm Snøhetta won the project—but not, it turned out, based on the design it produced.

The university had teamed students with each of the six architecture firms to develop designs. After observing how each firm worked, the selection committee was most impressed with Snøhetta, which demonstrated a collaborative and inclusive approach to design and built a rapport with the students and faculty.

When the university awarded the project to Snøhetta, it asked the firm to throw out the proposed design, which was a very traditional brick building with a circular tower. The university wanted a more modern and forward-looking building to support its forward-thinking mission.

The James B. Hunt Jr. Library is named after North Carolina's longest-serving governor, who helped define the library's technology-driven program with then-Director of Libraries Susan Nutter. With their input, the library includes a lab for the development of video games, a creativity studio, a 3D printing workshop, a submarine simulation center for ROTC training, and a special gallery for the Institute for Emerging Issues think tank.

[TOP] Stephen with former Governor James B. Hunt Jr.
[BOTTOM] Stephen with project architect Nic Rader of Snøhetta.

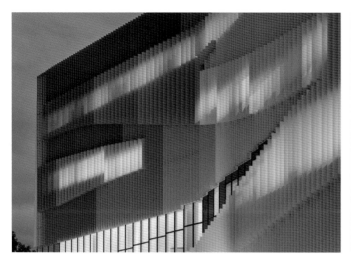

[FAR LEFT] View of the vertical fins and glass curtain wall facade. The curtain wall construction used over 800 different-sized panels to create the dazzling sculptural effect.

[LEFT] At night, the interior light reflects off the layers of metal fins to create a magical effect.

[LEFT, SECOND FROM TOP] Early computer rendering of the design.

[LEFT, SECOND FROM BOTTOM] Massing model of the James B. Hunt Library set in the campus context.

[LEFT, BOTTOM] Producer Dan Frank and Snøhetta's Nic Rader review the design concepts.

The library is a sleek metal box on the Centennial Campus, the university's research and engineering extension. Like much of Snøhetta's work, the design of the Hunt Library responds to the landscape.

The building's linear, sloping shape mirrors the topography, and one end of the building tilts up to direct views toward Lake Raleigh and downtown Raleigh. Instead of using the building to anchor the end of the quadrangle, the architects pushed the building to the side so that views of the lake would be shared throughout the campus.

Although Snøhetta and local architects Clark Nexsen used universal materials like steel and glass to evoke a modern feel, they looked to the history of the area to form their concept. Throughout the building, the architects reference the textile weaving industry of Raleigh. Walls of glass and metal panels intertwine on the exterior. Vertical sun-shading blades add another layer to be woven into the facade, creating an additional layer of visual interest. Together with fritted, or ceramic-patterned, glass, the vertical metal blades also form a simple but effective system to control the natural light that is desirable to people but harmful to books.

From the outside, the forms of the interior staircases can be read as paths weaving through the building. The vivid yellow stairs are the major organizing elements on the interior and are meant to encourage activity. Placed more prominently than the dark purple elevators, the stairs invite people to move through the building. As successful as they are in promoting walking, the staircases were designed for more than just moving up and down the building. They also promote interaction and conversation. Parts of the stairs widen into amphitheater-style seating for larger gatherings or built-in benches for smaller meetings.

[LEFT] Vibrant colors help to organize the interior and serve as a way-finding system.
[BELOW] Stephen and Craig Dykers of Snøhetta discuss the reasoning behind the over-scaled steps.

[RIGHT] Diagrams studying site and placement of the building on the campus setting.

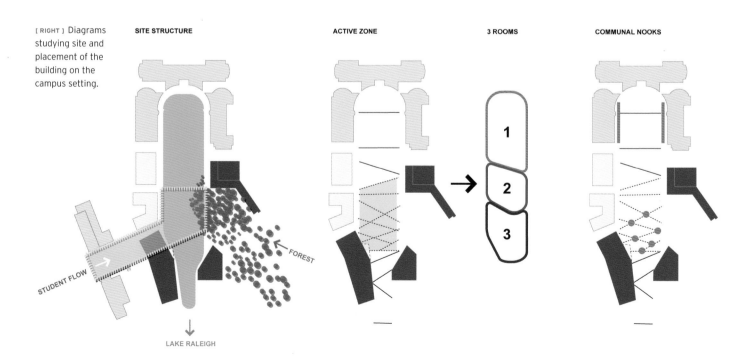

SITE STRUCTURE

STUDENT FLOW →

FOREST

↓ LAKE RALEIGH

ACTIVE ZONE

3 ROOMS

→

1

2

3

COMMUNAL NOOKS

[FAR TOP LEFT] Craig Dykers using twine to explain a building concept.
[FAR LEFT , SECOND FROM TOP] Built-in seating at stairs encourages social interaction.
[FAR LEFT , SECOND FROM BOTTOM] View of lighting lining the undersides of the stairs.
[FAR BOTTOM LEFT] Meeting spaces tucked into the stairs.
[LEFT] View from stair landing into main reading room.

The vertical stair sequence through the building culminates at the Skyline Reading Room, a bright, cheerful space for reading with a stunning backdrop of sky and lake. The room can also be seen from the rest of the university campus and acts as a beacon.

Historically, books have determined the layout of libraries by taking up most of the space and limiting the amount of light in the building. In the Hunt Library, however, people and ideas are the main features. Instead of densely packed bookshelves in poorly lit rooms, natural light and open spaces take priority. Large double-story areas with colorful seating surround book stacks and quieter study rooms so that the perimeter of the building can remain brightly lit and open to views outside.

The solution to efficiently storing books without infringing on meeting spaces also developed from the project's collaborative design process. When the design team and the university asked students for suggestions on the technology that the library should provide, the students stressed that whatever the technology, it should be user friendly.

The bookBot is an easy-to-use book search-and-retrieval system whose workings can be understood by watching it through its glass enclosure. The automated book-delivery system compressed the library's collections into less than a quarter of the space required by conventional shelving. The majority of the library's collections are held in the high-density storage area accessed solely by the Book-bot. This not only reduced shelf space but also eliminated the space needed to browse between shelves. The area that would normally be taken up by shelving could then be reallocated for meeting rooms, study spaces, studios, and other interaction areas.

Working with the students, faculty, and staff who would use the library, Snøhetta and Clark Nexsen designed a thrilling building that meets the social as well as academic needs of a modern university library. From concept to final structure, the James B. Hunt Jr. Library is a story of true collaboration that raised the profile of North Carolina State University with innovative and thoughtful design.

[BELOW] The "conventional" reading room with seating area that overlooks the lake.
[BOTTOM] Overview of the colorful main reading area.

[ABOVE] Snøhetta incorporated the bookBot—an automated book storage and retrieval system—into the library.

[ABOVE] Brightly lit main reading room on the main level.

[RIGHT] Interactive lounge with ever-changing display screens.

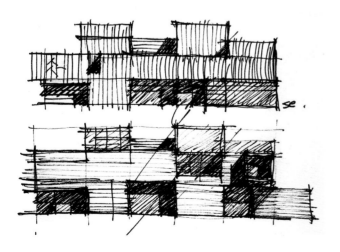

South Mountain Community Library

by Richärd+Bauer
Phoenix, Arizona

Libraries are not what they used to be. To survive the digital information and social media age, the quiet places that stored and dispensed knowledge have evolved into bustling hubs where people share and create information. Public libraries especially are revisiting their function as community centers, while academic libraries are incorporating functions usually belonging to coffee shops, lounges, and media laboratories.

The South Mountain Community Library, named for a mountain that sits within the city limits of Phoenix, presented the challenge of combining the new civic role of a public library with the educational needs of an academic library. The joint venture between the South Mountain Community College and the Phoenix Public Library system required one building to join the separate entities. The new building also presented the opportunity to create an oasis of sorts, a center for the community and an iconic building for the college.

To design a cohesive building with a modern identity, architects Richärd+Bauer combined the past with the future. The architects mined the area's history to connect the building with its community and looked to technology to shape its image.

Richärd+Bauer studied the agricultural history of Maricopa County and designed abstract patterns of asters, citrus, sorghum, and cotton, the region's four major crops. Inside the library, the architects used digital fabrication methods to apply their custom patterns onto laser-cut acrylic and waterjet-cut aluminum guardrails.

The architects were also inspired by integrated circuits, which they used as an organizing idea to arrange the functions in the building. After working out the distinct programs of the academic library and the public library, they grouped related spaces together and buffered them from unrelated functions, which is the basic concept of an integrated circuit.

The library is a two-story cube with extruded and recessed bars wrapped in shimmering copper. The bent planks of copper, an essential part of Arizona's industry, form a rainscreen that is an effective exterior cladding system that allows structures to

[TOP LEFT] Roof monitors seen from a distance.
[MIDDLE LEFT] Section through building looking east showing roof monitor volumes.
[BOTTOM LEFT] Section through building looking south.
[TOP RIGHT] Jim Richärd sketches the basic building concept.
[BOTTOM RIGHT] Massing model.

breathe by incorporating an air gap behind the outermost siding material. Because of Arizona's arid climate, the copper has deepened to a bronze tone instead of the typical green patina seen in most other climates.

The alternating glass and copper skin allows natural daylight into the library while allowing views out onto courtyards and gardens. The landscaping of the gardens and courtyards was carefully designed to incorporate indigenous plantings to further connect the library to the area.

Above the basic copper-and-glass-clad volumes, Richärd+Bauer placed five large roof monitors to bring even more natural light into the library. The roof monitors are popped-up extensions of the building with high windows, or clerestories. Because the glass is on the sides instead of overhead as in skylights, the monitors block direct sunlight while allowing diffuse natural light into the building. The monitors act as light wells during daytime and glow like lanterns in the evening. Patterns of fritted and colored glass based on agricultural patterns reinforce the concept of connecting the building to its site.

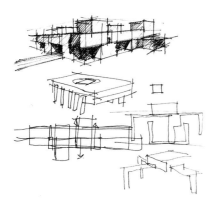

[TOP LEFT] Site model showing roof monitors.
[MIDDLE LEFT] Sketch studies by Jim Richärd.
[ABOVE] View from upper academic level and acoustic wood ceiling.
[LEFT] View of copper rainscreen showing bar code pattern.

[ABOVE] The library provides diverse seating and studying areas.

[LEFT] A mural printed on a chain link screen with printed pattern features young adults in various poses and serves to give the teen area privacy.

[ABOVE] View of laser cut guardrails and patterned glass of roof monitor windows.

[FAR RIGHT] Boardroom with cedar strip paneling and ceiling.

[RIGHT] Stephen with Toni Garvey, the former Phoenix librarian who championed the South Mountain Community Library project.

To organize the dueling functions, the design team placed the public spaces such as meeting rooms, multipurpose room, children's area, and cybercafé on the ground floor, and the academic group study rooms, non-fiction collections, special collections, quiet study rooms, and classrooms on the upper level. Clearly separating the functions allowed the design team to concentrate on shaping interaction spaces around the vertical circulation areas.

The college and community leaders of Maricopa County wanted to promote interaction and connection between students and neighbors. To create places where people would feel comfortable interacting, Richärd+Bauer expanded the patterned aluminum guardrails on the stair landings to form landing pods. The landing pods occur where people would naturally meet and provide semi-private seating areas.

Richärd+Bauer ensured that any visitor whether student or local citizen would feel comfortable in the library by designing very open spaces that were easy to understand and easy to navigate. Since modern glass-and-metal finishes can make spaces feel cold, the architects used wood on the ceilings and walls to create warmth. The overall effect is a bright, welcoming space that is tied to its context.

Accommodating both local residents and college students, the South Mountain Community Library is an elegant design solution to a complex challenge. The stunning building, a publicly supported project, is a symbol of investing in the community and inspires pride. With a respectful study of place and imaginative applications of common materials, Richärd+Bauer designed a beautiful building that successfully brings a community together.

[TOP] Stephen and Kelly Bauer in a landing pod.
[ABOVE] View of main floor lobby.

On Performance Spaces

Roger K. Lewis, FAIA

Performance spaces can be cool and inspiring. Artfully designed structures for music, theater, and dance engage all our senses. I love creating performance architecture because it offers an expressive aesthetic potential most architectural commissions lack.

My first opportunity to build for performance came soon after architecture school. A Peace Corps volunteer in Tunisia, I designed several civic auditoriums. Thirty years later, I was the design competition professional adviser for the University of Maryland's performing arts center. A decade after that, I co-chaired the building committee for the new Woolly Mammoth Theatre in Washington, D.C.

Architecture can be likened to frozen music or even dancing forms, suddenly frozen. "Frozen music" describes the richly ornamented facades and interior surfaces enveloping the grand spaces of the 19th century Paris Opera House, designed by Charles Garnier. Forms frozen in movement characterize the Jørn Utzon's Sydney Opera House, Frank Gehry's Walt Disney Concert Hall, in Los Angeles, and Santiago Calatrava's Tenerife Auditorium, in the Canary Islands.

The Paris Opera House and Disney Hall each contain a performance space within, but the shapes of the interior houses are not telegraphed to the exterior. The overall geometry and skin of the Barclays Center, in Brooklyn, designed by SHoP Architects, and the Arena Stage in Washington, D.C., designed by Bing Thom, do not reflect the shapes of performance spaces inside. Likewise, in dense urban settings, performance spaces are deeply embedded within street-fronting buildings abutting other buildings. At Carnegie Hall in Manhattan and Broadway-style theaters in Boston, Chicago, and San Francisco, patrons experience visual delight not outside, but rather within lobbies and performance spaces.

Performance spaces necessitate clear-span structural systems over audience, stage, and backstage areas to support floors or roofs above, plus catwalks, ductwork, piping, electrical conduits, lighting, acoustic panels, scenery, and ceilings. In downtown theaters, clear-span structural members are usually unexpressed. But in freestanding edifices like the Sydney Opera House or Tenerife Auditorium, creatively marrying structural skeleton, exterior shell, and interior volume is a primary source of aesthetic expression.

Yet shaping a good performance space is not just about aesthetics. Performance and audience demands are paramount. Seats need unobstructed sight lines enabling audience members to see performers as well as other audience members. Good acoustic characteristics enable voices and musical instruments to be heard clearly without distortion at all frequencies. Interior spaces must be environmentally comfortable, tempered by quiet, draft-free, thermally balanced, energy-efficient HVAC systems.

The ideal performance space is single-purpose. Multi-purpose spaces rarely serve any single purpose well because vital spatial attributes are unavoidably compromised and sub-optimum for each purpose. A concert hall doesn't work for opera, nor an opera house for chamber music or orchestral works. Theaters seating 2,000 can be grand, but lack the intimacy of theaters seating a few hundred. Thus, the best performing arts venues encompass distinctly separate, diversified spaces, each custom-shaped, sized and engineered.

Contemplate the quality of the structure and space housing the next performance you attend. You may appreciate why architecture can be a performing art.

Roger K. Lewis, FAIA, *is a practicing architect, planner, author, and journalist. He writes the "Shaping the City" column in* The Washington Post *and is professor emeritus of planning and preservation at the University of Maryland School of Architecture. Roger serves as a trustee for the National Children's Museum and as president and director of the Peace Corps Commemorative Foundation.*

Performance Spaces

[ABOVE] View of retracting end zone doors from a plaza. When the doors are opened it is possible to see from one end zone plaza to the other.

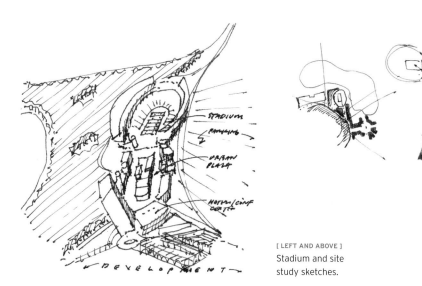

[LEFT AND ABOVE] Stadium and site study sketches.

Dallas Cowboys Stadium

by HKS Architects
Arlington, Texas

Given its informal motto, "everything is bigger in Texas," it's no surprise that the Lone Star State is home to one of the largest sports and entertainment arenas in the world.

Dallas Cowboys Stadium is a checklist of the world's largest built elements, including the world's largest retractable roof, retracting doors, column-free structure, and high-definition television screens. The home field of the most-watched football team in the United States is a quarter of a mile long.

The personality of the man behind the football team is just as large as the stadium. To bring his vision for a world-class sports center to reality, Jerry Jones wanted a firm that would take his ideas seriously. The new stadium would be the largest physical symbol of the team and needed to enhance the Dallas Cowboys brand that Jones and his family had helped to build and maintain. Jones chose the local Dallas office of HKS Architects.

A major goal of the project was to entice people to leave the comforts of their homes and join their fellow fans at a live event. The building needed to provide an experience that fans couldn't begin to approach at home, even with surround-sound entertainment systems.

[BELOW] The arch trusses sit on massive concrete abutments at each end of the stadium.

[RIGHT] Each arch truss is 35 feet deep by 17 feet wide and 1,225 feet long.

[BOTTOM] Sketches studying form and structure.

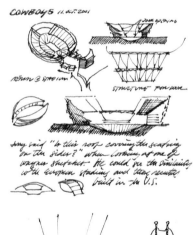

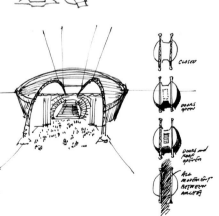

The team's solution was to present entertainment on a monumental scale. To transform the entire activity of attending a live football game into an event, the design team designed plazas around the building so that fans walk through landscaped paths instead of huge expanses of parking lots. The plazas create a sense of ceremony and arrival and provide civic spaces where visitors can rest, picnic, or tailgate.

For the building itself, the design team was inspired by the strength and energy of football and wanted to express power and motion through structure. Two immense arch trusses soar above the field and support a translucent domed roof. The 1,225-foot-long arches continue through the glass end walls and are anchored by huge concrete supports.

The choice between a conventional grid of pillars or clear span arches was easy. The design team went further in highlighting the structure by using glass everywhere. Sloping glass walls, retractable glass doors at the end zones, and a large band of glass at the roof edge provide clear views of the arches and of the field.

The former stadium, Texas Stadium, featured a signature hole in the roof, and HKS Architects repeated the gesture to pay homage. The roof of the Dallas Cowboys Stadium is covered in a translucent Teflon-coated material that transmits 12 percent of natural light. Designed to open or close in 12 minutes, it is the longest single-span roof structure in the world. When the roof is open, the entire field is visible from above.

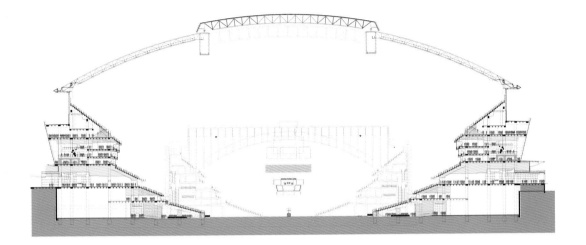

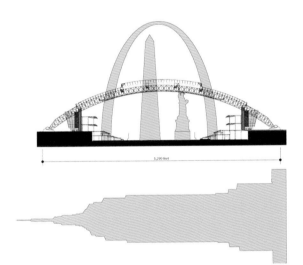

1,290 feet

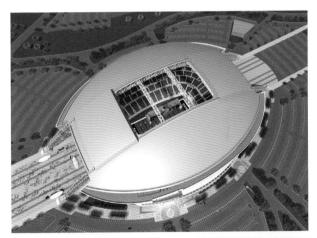

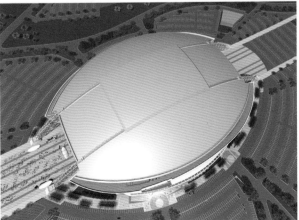

[ABOVE] Diagram comparing the size of Dallas Cowboys stadium to other American landmarks. The entire Statue of Liberty and its base could fit into the stadium with the roof closed.
[RIGHT] Brian Trubey of HKS Architects demonstrates the software used to design the stadium.

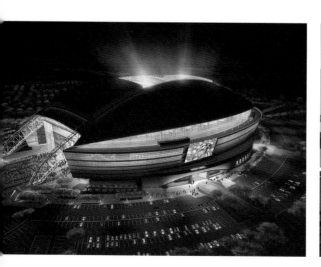

[ABOVE] One of the most compelling architectural features of the stadium design is the canted glass exterior wall, which slopes outward at a 14 degree angle.

[FAR LEFT] Nighttime rendering.

[LEFT] Rendering of the arches and retractable end zone doors. Each end entrance is 120 feet high by 180 feet wide. The five 38-foot-long panels take only 6 minutes to open or close.

[TOP] Fans enjoy watching the action from the screens spanning between the 20 yard lines.
[ABOVE] Filming the world's largest video screens.

[ABOVE RIGHT] Stephen with Bryan Trubey, principal designer at HKS.
[BELOW] Section through the seating bowl and playing field, which are 50 feet below street level.

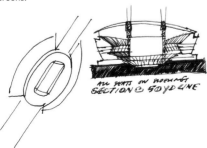

To compete with home theater technology, Jones wanted the stadium to provide a great view from any seat, whether in the highest tiers of general admission or in the field level luxury suites. Hanging approximately 90 feet above the field is a video display with the world's largest high-definition screens. Extending from one 20-yard line to the other, the screens provide a larger than life view of the action on the field to spectators at every level.

Inside the stadium, HKS rearranged the traditional stadium seating to free up the end zones. The architects stacked seating tiers higher and limited the seating areas to between the goal lines. Luxury suites were also stacked instead of alternating between tiers of seating, where they have typically been placed. A special field level of suites, called dugout suites, were added to get fans closer to the players on the field. All of these moves opened up the end zones, where the architects placed flexible concourses that could be used for standing-room-only areas during major events like the Super

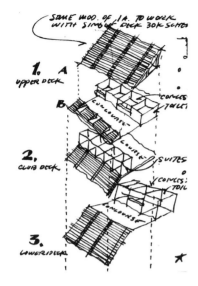

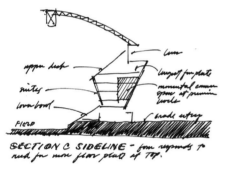

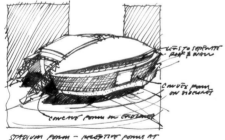

[TOP] Sketches diagramming
seating tiers.
[CENTER] Sketch of
seating and circulation
on the sidelines.
[ABOVE] Sketch of the
final form of the Stadium.

Bowl. Normally the end zones are open to views of the plazas, which is a unique feature for a football stadium.

Building the new stadium was priority No. 1 for the entire Jones family, and they gave as much attention to the gigantic project as they would to a home renovation. The Joneses became serious students of architecture and toured other stadiums and buildings recommended by their architects. The family found inspiration from the tours, all the way down to epoxy flooring and silverware for the club dining room.

Gene Jones, Jerry Jones' wife, felt the space was not complete without art. With her daughter Charlotte, she created a public art program for the stadium that commissioned original pieces by contemporary artists. The custom artwork displayed throughout the stadium make world-class art available to the community.

We've seen architecture used as a marketing tool before, but Dallas Cowboys Stadium employed architecture to strengthen a brand. Led by a team effort by the Jones family, the stadium represents the power of a sport, the worldwide reach of an American football team, and a higher level of entertainment.

[ABOVE LEFT] Stephen with Dallas Cowboys cheerleaders.

[ABOVE RIGHT] Stephen with Charlotte Jones, who spearheaded the stadium's public arts program with her mother, Gene Jones.

[BELOW] Luxury clubroom of the Cowboys Stadium.

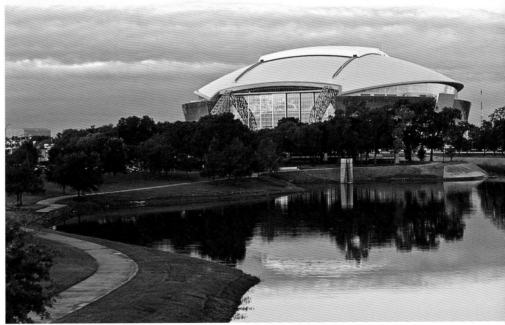

Kauffman Center for the Performing Arts

by Moshe Safdie Architects
Kansas City, Missouri

The Kauffman Center for the Performing Arts houses the Kansas City Symphony, the Lyric Opera, and the Kansas City Ballet in one iconic building, providing spaces specifically designed according to the types of performances. Aside from New York's Lincoln Center and Washington, D.C.'s Kennedy Center, the Kauffman Center is the only other event space in the United States that contains two designated performance halls under one roof.

The center was named in honor of Muriel McBrien Kauffman, a Kansas City philanthropist and civic leader who passed away in 1995. Kauffman believed in creating a strong arts and culture program to establish Kansas City as a cosmopolitan center. After her death, Kauffman's daughter Julia took over the family's charitable foundation and fulfilled her mother's mission to create a performance space that would attract world-famous talent.

[ABOVE LEFT] Sketch showing the glass tent connecting the performance halls.
[ABOVE CENTER] Sketch of arced forms of the performance halls.
[ABOVE RIGHT] Concept sketches of the performance hall spaces.

[RIGHT] Stephen with Moshe Safdie, architect of the Kauffman Center for the Performing Arts.
[FAR RIGHT] Safdie designed the building to have no front or back, so that the surrounding city enjoys dramatic views of the Center from all directions.

[LEFT] Stephen explaining the tensile structural system.

[LEFT, SECOND FROM TOP] View of the cables at the glass roof.

[LEFT, SECOND FROM BOTTOM] Julia Kauffman with project architect Isaac Franco.

[LEFT, BOTTOM] Crew filming next to the stainless steel and precast concrete arcs.

[RIGHT] Site plan showing the performance halls located next to each other.

[BELOW] The rhythm of cables is meant to evoke musical instruments.

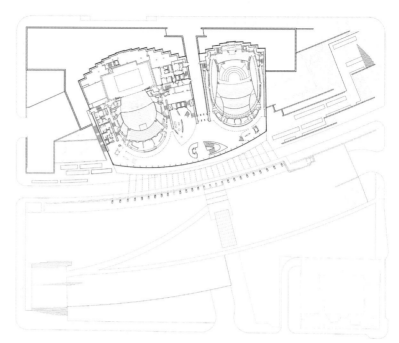

[LEFT] The balconies from both performance halls are visible through the dramatically sloping glass walls.

[ABOVE] Balconies create a grand theater experience in Brandmeyer Great Hall. [BELOW] Sketch showing the balconies visible through glass "tent" structure.

To raise the cultural profile of Kansas City, the Kauffmans saw the need for an iconic building that would draw attention to the city. Putting their money behind their civic-minded ideals, the Kauffmans led the way to funding the building entirely with private donations. The successful fundraising campaign underscored the deep pride and commitment of the local community.

Massachusetts-based Moshe Safdie Architects was chosen from an impressive list of internationally acclaimed design firms to create a landmark that would solidify the city's growing cultural reputation. Like a scene out of a movie, the architect sketched the basic design concept on a napkin during a dinner with his clients.

The building is a simple organization of two curving forms enclosing the performance halls and a glass tent-like structure over a grand lobby. The two performance halls are on the north side of the site. Becaues the halls are inward focused, Safdie designed them as solid, sculptural elements. In contrast, the lobby is faced with a curving, canted glass wall and cable system. The distinct curved forms of the performance halls and the glass tent with strands of steel cables evoke musical instruments.

opaque - transparent -

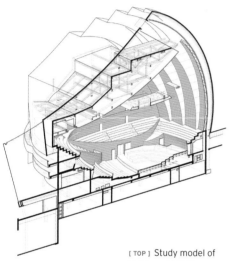

The glass-enclosed foyer, Brandmeyer Great Hall, was designed as a porch where patrons could see and be seen. Balconies and a sweeping staircase echo the grand experience of traditional theaters, allowing patrons to display themselves and check out other theatergoers. The neutral tones of the interior walls act like backdrops for which people provide the color and energy.

Dramatically angled outward, the glass walls and roof are supported by a tensile structural system of masts and cables. The line of cables supporting the glass roof leans over the drop-off roadway and creates a modern version of a marquee.

In contrast, the enclosures of the performance halls conceal their structural systems, which are formed by a series of curved steel trusses with a similar radius. The trusses fan out from each other and rotate around the performance areas. On the exterior, warm-toned precast concrete clads the vertical inner rims of the arcs, while stainless steel clads the outer curved faces.

Helzberg Hall is the designated residence for the Kansas City Symphony. Safdie wanted a connection between the exterior and interior forms and expressed the arcs in the space. Working with Yasuhisa Toyota of Nagata Acoustics, the arcs were backed with sound-absorbing materials to provide an acoustically pleasing space.

Where the arcs on the outside fan to reveal limestone sides, the arcs in Helzberg Hall split to create skylights. Bringing in natural light is an unusual move for a performance space, but the dramatically high ceilings and well-coordinated acoustics allow the brightness to feel natural. Safdie and Toyota placed audience members on all sides of

[TOP] Study model of Helzberg Hall. The tallest point of the room is approximately 100 feet above the stage.
[ABOVE] Drawing of a section through Helzberg Hall showing structure and seating.
[RIGHT] Stephen and Isaac Franco on the stage of Helzberg Hall. Douglas fir and Alaskan yellow cedar were chosen for their acoustic properties.

[RIGHT] Interior view of Helzberg Hall. Skylights between the fanning arcs light the organ.

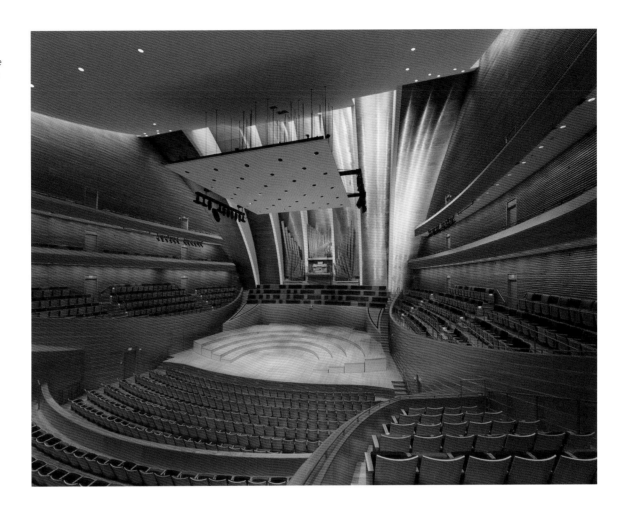

[FAR LEFT] Exterior of the acoustic model of Helzberg Hall.
[LEFT] Acoustic model of Helzberg Hall.

[ABOVE] Detailed
acoustic model of
the Muriel Kauffman
Theatre.

[ABOVE] Stage of
the Muriel Kauffman
Theatre.
[BELOW] Sketch showing
structural concept of the
performance spaces.

[RIGHT] Horseshoe
shaped balcony tiers
of the Muriel Kauffman
Theatre.

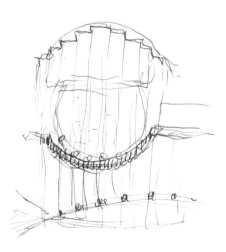

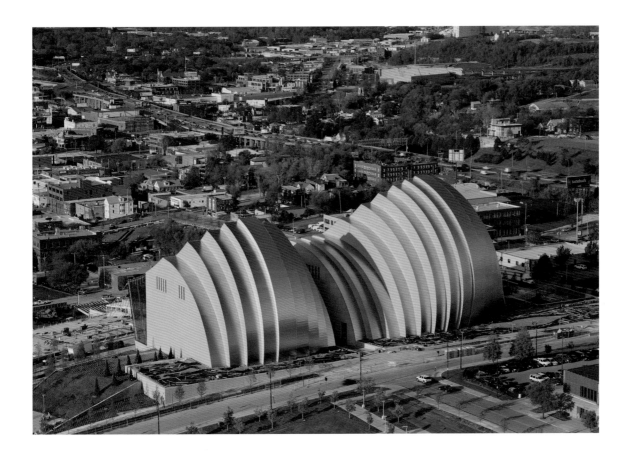

the stage in an arena seating format instead of traditional tiered balcony seating. The arrangement created a single volume of space equally shared by the audience, who surround the musicians instead of facing them.

Taking a cue from the great European opera houses, the Muriel Kauffman Theatre feels more like a traditional theater space, with three tiers of balcony seating and dark colors. Home to the Kansas City Ballet and the Lyric Opera of Kansas City, the theater's form rotates the nested arcs of the exterior. Safdie and Toyota shaped the walls to follow the horseshoe shapes of the balcony tiers. Murals designed by students of the Kansas City Art Institute decorate and disguise the acoustic baffles. To create a special, twinkling quality of light, Safdie designed guardrails incorporating lights and a Mylar film to create glimmering tiers of balconies.

To honor the legacy of Muriel McBrien Kauffman's commitment to the arts and the community of Kansas City, Safdie designed a building meant to stand out and stand apart. The iconic form of the Kauffman Center for the Performing Arts establishes Kansas City as a cultural player on the international stage.

[ABOVE] Model of the final form of the Kauffman Center.

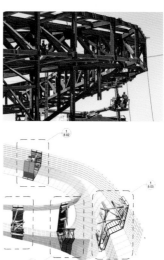

Barclays Center

by SHoP Architects with AECOM
Brooklyn, New York

The new home of the Brooklyn Nets and the future home of the New York Islanders is more than just a sports arena. Designed by SHoP Architects, Barclays Center is also a concert arena, mass transit stop, public plaza, and the beginning of the Atlantic Yards development. As the first part of a massive 22-acre development, the new arena was to be the crown jewel. While most new arenas focus inward, Barclays Center reaches out and engages its neighborhood.

The developer of the Atlantic Yards, Bruce Ratner, went straight to sports arena experts Ellerbe Beckett, now AECOM. Ratner had admired one of the firm's previous arenas and asked it to repeat the design for his Brooklyn site. The resulting design, an arched roof stadium clad in brick, gave him the basic bones of the project. But Ratner had a grander vision: He wanted to make an exciting architectural statement that would relate to the urban neighborhood. Based on a recommendation from an architect friend, Ratner hired SHoP Architects. He charged the firm with creating a design that would capture the excitement of a new team set in a rapidly changing area, but still feel as though it belonged in Brooklyn.

[OPPOSITE FAR LEFT AND TOP RIGHT] Photo of the construction of the oculus.
[OPPOSITE, BOTTOM RIGHT] Drawing of detailed construction modeling.
[ABOVE LEFT] Stephen with Bruce Ratner, chairman and CEO of the development company responsible for the Barclays Center.
[ABOVE RIGHT] Stephen with Gregg Pasquarelli, a principal of ShoP Architects.

[ABOVE LEFT] Photo of the metal lattice under construction.
[ABOVE] View of the glass walls at street level that allow passersby to see the activities in the center.
[FAR LEFT] Detail view showing the open weave pattern of the pre-weathered steel panels.
[LEFT] Street view of Barclays Center at night.

Since the basic interior building shape was already set, SHoP Architects worked out a dynamic skin to cover the guts of the stadium designed by AECOM. The architects designed a bulging, warping lattice-like wrapper to transform the basic box into something more dynamic. The lattice is made with pre-weathered steel panels that were chosen specifically to match the rusty tones of nearby Brooklyn brownstones.

At the main entrance, the designers stretched the steel lattice upward to create a 30-foot-high overhead canopy. Extending 85 feet out from the main structure, the canopy defines a public plaza and features a large opening, or oculus. The oculus is roughly the size of a basketball court and presents a grand civic gesture. Within the entire circumference of its inner rim is a band of continuously changing LED signage.

Barclays Center is one of the only true urban venues in the United States with no dedicated parking and sits on one of the busiest intersections of the New York subway system. Most visitors arrive from the underground station and take escalators directly into the entry plaza. The oculus and its video band are best experienced from this perspective.

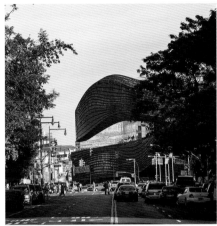

[ABOVE LEFT] View of the grand canopy and opening, or oculus.
[ABOVE RIGHT] View approaching the busy intersection in front of the Barclays Center.
[LEFT] View of the LED video band within the inner circumference of the oculus.

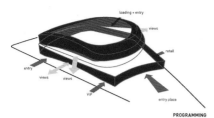

PROGRAMMING

CIVIC GESTURE

[ABOVE] Concept diagrams of the building design.
[BELOW] Diagram of the two main components of the exterior form: the halo and the canopy.

CANOPY

HALO

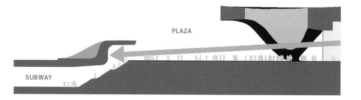

PLAZA

SUBWAY

[ABOVE] View of the oculus from the public transportation exit.
[LEFT] Section drawing showing the clear view from the subway exits through the Center.
[BELOW] Diagrammatic section showing relationships of the street, seating, arena floor, and suites.

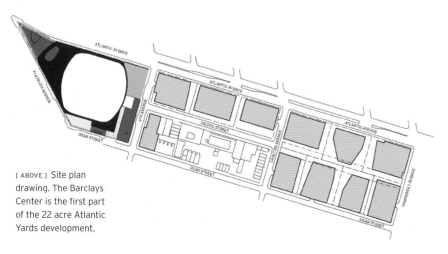

[ABOVE] Site plan drawing. The Barclays Center is the first part of the 22 acre Atlantic Yards development.

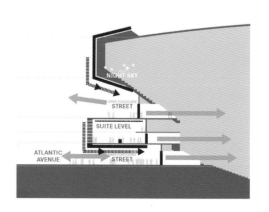

SHoP Architects designed the arena to be very transparent on the street level, so that people walking by could see all the activity inside the center, including the main event floor. The design team had placed the event level one story below grade to create a sunken bowl. A band of glass splits the metal lattice and circles the entire sidewalk level to offer dramatic views of the events inside. Sinking the main event space below street level also reduced the height so that the scale of the building did not overwhelm its residential surroundings.

The experience of attending a game or concert at Barclays Center was carefully choreographed to be an exciting event. Visitors first see the event floor or the players' practice court from the outside and get a glimpse of the dramatic seating bowl. Once inside, fans see the scoreboard and walk down to their seats in a dark, theater-like setting. The seating tiers are raked, or sloped, at the sharpest angle safely allowed. The steep angles reduce the distance between the fans and the event floor and also allow for a narrower building footprint.

[ABOVE] Stephen plays one on one with Gregg.
[BELOW] View of the sunken bowl seating and event floor.

[LEFT] View of one of the bars in the center.

[RIGHT] Stephen with Chris Sharples, a principal of ShoP Architects, in the ShoP office.
[FAR RIGHT] Highpoint Solutions lounge and bar.
[BELOW LEFT] A concourse of local retailers is open even when there are no events.
[BOTTOM RIGHT] View of the court level VIP champagne lounge with shimmering metal screens.

To create a feeling of intimacy, the designers lowered the height of the original arched roof structure so that fans would feel as if they were sitting up in the rafters of the roof. As in any modern sports arena, the Barclays Center also incorporated touches of luxury. Krista Ninivaggi, SHoP's director of interiors, brought the exterior motifs in lighter color and materials inside the arena. Working closely with the rapper and then-part owner, Jay Z, the firm introduced gold, bright white, and deeply saturated color schemes into the clubs, bars, and restaurants.

During the construction of the project, SHoP Architects employed digital fabrication at the highest level. The firm had developed a proprietary app that allowed the project team, including the owner, to watch the delivery and installation process in real time. The fabrication and system-based approach to design is a SHoP trademark and helped the client bring the project to reality in a shorter than standard amount of time.

Using industrial materials and a high level of transparency, SHoP Architects designed the Barclays Center to connect to the neighborhood streets. The thrilling entertainment space is a modern landmark for Brooklyn.

On Cool Spaces

George Thrush, FAIA
Director, Northeastern University School of Architecture

When I heard that my friend Stephen Chung was producing a program about architecture, I was delighted. In our profession, we have long lacked an accessible way for the public to understand what we do. Of course there have been programs about the homes of the rich and famous, but these shows tend to imply that architecture is only about excess, gaudy finishes, and over-the-top features. A viewer of such shows could easily get the impression that architecture is simply a way to make things cost more!

But *Cool Spaces!* is much more than that. Stephen's show welcomes viewers in to a world where architects and designers are solving real problems. And this is why Northeastern University is happy to be involved. At the Northeastern University School of Architecture, we are dedicated to raising problem solving to the level of art, not creating idiosyncratic new forms in the hope that they might possibly address a real need. And *Cool Spaces!* provides a unique window into this design process.

The interrelationship between problem solving, composition, material, and style is one that has been around for a long time. It's a variation on the old "form versus function" discussion, and it will likely always be with us. But solving real problems has never been more important. We face enormous challenges in designing today's cities—among them, environmental imperatives that demand a much higher level of awareness about energy consumption and use of resources.

Today's challenges require sustainable solutions, and many architects are coming up with innovative approaches to recurring problems. So it makes sense that *Cool Spaces!* organizes its episodes according to the type of problem being solved—healing spaces, performances spaces, education spaces, and so on.

This kind of comprehensive study of innovation in architecture and design is also central to preparing our young people for the future. It allows them to learn from people who are the core innovators in our country—people who understand the need to question assumptions and challenge the way we do things.

Indeed, I now teach a large course called Understanding Design that is open to all Northeastern students and available for viewing by the general public (find it online at http://tinyurl.com/understandingdesign). It focuses on the commonality of design approaches across multiple disciplines, so that young people, no matter their area of study, can learn the importance of this mode of inquiry.

So it shouldn't be surprising that our School of Architecture happily agreed to join *Cool Spaces!* on its mission to educate the larger public about the value that good design brings to our world. This will have a real impact on both young people during their educational years and their parents as they make decisions that will shape the future of our entire shared environment.

In other words, it couldn't be a more important task.

George Thrush *is the director of the School of Architecture at Northeastern University, in Boston. George's published pieces include "Ring City: Civic Liberalism and Urban Design" and "Boston's New Urban Ring: An Antidote to Fragmentation." He received his Bachelor of Architecture from the University of Tennessee and his Master of Architecture from Harvard University. In 2005, George was named to the American Institute of Architects College of Fellows.*

Healing Spaces

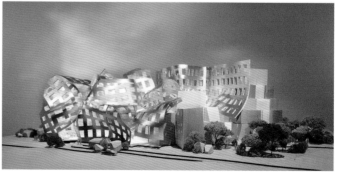

Lou Ruvo Center for Brain Health

by Gehry Partners
Las Vegas, Nevada

The Lou Ruvo Center for Brain Health reveals the serious side of Sin City. Located a mile north of the glitzy hotels and casinos on the Las Vegas Strip, the modestly scaled building is designed by one of the world's most famous architects.

Frank O. Gehry is as close as it gets to a celebrity architect. The prolific designer is friends with actors like Brad Pitt, boasts a guest appearance on *The Simpsons*, has a namesake condominium building in Manhattan, and is the architect of perhaps the most celebrated building of the past generation: the Guggenheim Museum in Bilbao, Spain.

In the enviable position of being able to pick his projects, Gehry had refused previous requests to design buildings in Las Vegas. He agreed to design the Lou Ruvo Center for two reasons: an almost immediate rapport with the client, Larry Ruvo, and the opportunity to contribute to the mission of the building.

Ruvo and Gehry bonded over shared losses of loved ones to degenerative brain diseases. Ruvo's father had passed away after suffering from Alzheimer's, and Gehry had lost one of his best friends to Huntington's disease.

Ruvo wanted to build a medical center with enough flair to attract a top-flight research organization. His extensive experience in the beverage business taught him the importance of packaging and marketing, and he saw architecture as a "necessary" marketing tool. A serious building by a serious architect would demonstrate commitment to curing diseases and the financial backing to support the work. For his part, Gehry stipulated that he would design the project only if Huntington's was added to the list of diseases the center would research.

Once the client found his architect, he began his search for a research institution to occupy and operate the center. When Gehry joined the project as the architect, his participation underscored the commitment to making a world-class clinic. Ruvo was then able to recruit one of the top medical directors in the field from the University of California, Los Angeles and bring in the renowned Cleveland Clinic to operate the facility.

The center, officially called the Cleveland Clinic's Lou Ruvo Center for Brain Health, is named for Larry Ruvo's father. The center provides outpatient treatment and conducts research for Alzheimer's, Parkinson's, Huntington's, multiple sclerosis, and ALS (Lou Gehrig's disease).

Gehry designed two contrasting wings to house the two arms of the center: the research and treatment clinic at the north end, and an event space, to be used specifically for fundraising, at the south end. The wings connect through an outdoor breezeway covered with a trellis.

[ABOVE] Discussing the concept of "medical tourism" with with David Baird, director of the UNLV School of Architecture.

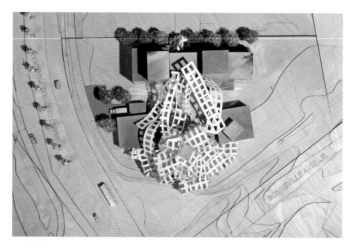

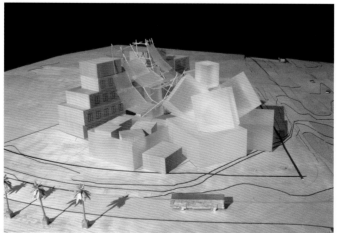

[LEFT] Overhead view of a progress model showing how the two sides are joined together.
[BELOW] Progress model showing the development of two contrasting wings.
[OPPOSITE, TOP] Ruvo Center construction under way.
[OPPOSITE, BOTTOM LEFT] Gehry sketch of curving skin and windows.
[OPPOSITE, BOTTOM RIGHT] The production team preps the remote control helicopters for aerial shots of the building.

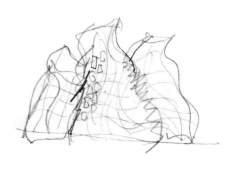

[LEFT] Stephen and production team shoot in front of the trellised breezeway connecting the medical office building and the event space.

[ABOVE, TOP] Model of the medical office wing.
[ABOVE, BOTTOM] The medical office wing was inspired by Moroccan hillside villages.
[BELOW] Model of the breezeway.

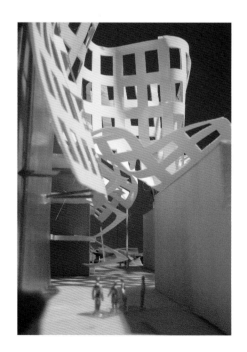

The four-story clinical wing houses medical offices, patient rooms, research space, and the headquarters of Ruvo's nonprofit foundation, Keep Memory Alive. The stacked white boxes that make up the office and clinical wing subtly mimic the surrounding cliffs. Gehry wanted to create a warm interior environment that did not resemble a medical setting, so he used honey-toned wood for all doors, trim, and furniture. In public areas, he also lightened the mood by installing many of his signature, free-form light fixtures. The clinical areas feature curved paths to control views and shield patients in different stages of illness from each other. The carefully laid out corridors also protect privacy.

The office wing appears rational and simple, especially next to the sculptural form of the event space, named the Life Activity Center. The relationship between the two forms reflects the relationship between the research organization and the nonprofit that supports it.

[TOP LEFT] The undulating structure and skin create a theatrical space with deeply recessed windows. [ABOVE] Interior model showing the tree trunk-like structural supports. [BELOW] Model of the outdoor entry area.

[LEFT] Producer Dan Frank interviews a volunteer at the clinic.
[BELOW, LEFT] Stephen with current and former mayors of Las Vegas, Carolyn and Oscar Goodman.
[BELOW] The curvilinear stainless steel skin incorporates 199 unique windows.

[ABOVE] Stephen explains how the exterior cladding was installed.
[RIGHT] Larry Ruvo hosts a winter dinner event.

The auditorium is primarily a fundraising space. Available to the public for rent, proceeds from Life Activity Center events help fund the center's research functions.

Tucked behind the white cliff side of the clinical wing, the Life Activity Center features a signature Gehry sculptural, metal-clad roof. The complex form is supported by a very precise structure that took 65,000 hours of engineering. The large number of unique steel pieces and connection points allowed no room for error.

Eighteen thousand stainless steel shingles and 199 unique windows make up the undulating facade. To form the outer layer, individual sheets of stainless steel were laid out on waterproofed plywood that enclosed the structure and created the shape of the roof. A grid was drawn onto the formwork so that metal sheets could be shaped and measured. The sheets were fabricated to fit into each other and to be installed sequentially. The final finish of the stainless steel was hand-scoured to reduce the glare of the untreated metal in the bright Nevada sun.

Celebrity is often used to bring attention to humanitarian causes, and Ruvo believed in the influence of Gehry's architecture. The Lou Ruvo Center for Brain Health showcases the power of architecture to attract, connect, and communicate.

SECTION 1- LOOKING NORTH

SECTION 2 LOOKING NORTH

SECTION 3 LOOKING WEST

Health Sciences Education Building

by CO Architects with Ayers Saint Gross
Phoenix, Arizona

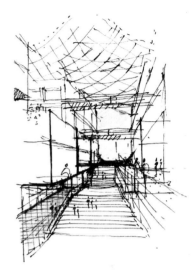

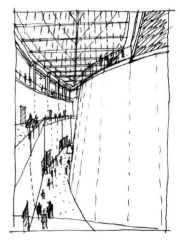

[ABOVE] Sketches of interaction spaces.

The Health Sciences Education Building anchors the Phoenix Biomedical Campus, a collaborative education and research campus in downtown Phoenix. The combined effort between the University of Arizona College of Medicine Phoenix and Northern Arizona University is an interdisciplinary teaching facility. The Health Sciences Education Building merges health education programs that typically have been taught separately. Modeled after a hospital, the program mirrors the reality of the healthcare industry in which physicians, nurses, and assistants work together.

Since team building is part of the building's program, the universities needed a design that would encourage teamwork. Working from a master plan developed by Ayers Saint Gross, Los Angeles-based CO Architects designed common areas throughout the new building where students from different programs could interact. The architects also created social spaces that encouraged serendipitous meetings among students, faculty, and staff. A central social space, called the mixing bar, houses shared and public functions such as the library, cafeteria, and student lounges. The mixing bar is organized around a central staircase set into a glass atrium at one end of what is the core of the building: the slot canyon.

[OPPOSITE, BOTTOM] Stacking diagram of the interdisciplinary programs.
[ABOVE LEFT] Stephen with Paul Zajfen, principal designer of CO Architects, below the rooftop sails of the slot canyon.

[RIGHT] View of students in a lecture hall.
[BELOW] Anatomy laboratory.
[BELOW RIGHT] Stephen interviews a medical student on a stair landing.

[BOTTOM LEFT] The Health Sciences Education Building contains flexible classrooms, simulation laboratories, gross anatomy facilities, pre-clinical training facilities, learning resources center, student services, faculty offices, and administrative spaces.
[BOTTOM RIGHT] Sketch by Paul Zajfen of the mixing bar staircases.

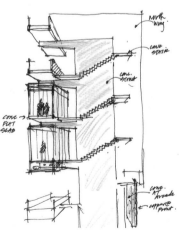

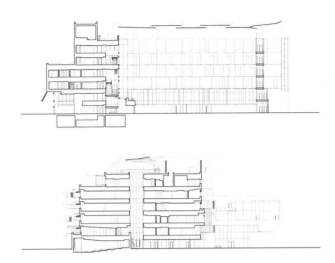

Arizona's intense climate called for a building that responded to the desert sunlight and extreme temperature swings. The Health Sciences Education Building's slot canyon is a tall, narrow courtyard that cuts through the main mass of the six-story building. It is modeled on the slot canyons that are naturally created by wind and water in the Sonora Desert. Since the tall, canted walls of slot canyons create their own shade, the spaces maintain temperatures 15-25 degrees cooler than the ambient outside temperatures. CO Architects applied the dramatic form and environmental concept of the naturally cooled shelters to the Health Sciences Education Building.

Following extensive daylight and solar studies, the architects shaped the building to provide optimal thermal and energy performance. The academic wings flanking the canyon bow in and out to create shade. To maximize the amount of daylight that would reach each wing, the depth of the wings were limited to 70 feet. A larger number of windows were placed at the lower level of the canyon and fewer windows at the top.

[ABOVE LEFT] View of the angled walls of the slot canyon.
[ABOVE RIGHT] Section drawing through the length of the slot canyon.
[ABOVE MIDDLE] Section view across the slot canyon.
[ABOVE] Sketch of mixing bar by Paul Zajfen.

[ABOVE] The copper panels on the south facade create canopies, seen at lower right.

Light-colored concrete block forms the walls of the courtyard canyon and provides a cool thermal mass. The thermal mass, a passive solar design strategy, stores the sun's heat energy during the day in its dense material. As the temperature drops at night, the walls slowly release the stored heat.

Teflon canopies at the roof further shield the canyon from direct overhead sun. The team of architects and engineers also designed the canyon to be conditioned with the exhaust air from the building's heating and cooling systems since the temperature of the exhaust air is lower than the temperature of the outside air.

[RIGHT] Street view showing the canyon inspired forms.
[BELOW] Production team shooting in front of the Health Siences Education Building.
[BELOW RIGHT] View of the mixing bar at the floor of the slot canyon courtyard.

For the exterior skin, CO Architects continued the motif of the Arizona landscape. They developed copper panels with folded patterns that mimic the stripes and grooves of the canyons and the saguaro cactus. The architects chose copper for the panels because the material allows heat to pass through quickly. Copper can also easily be formed and stretched into complex, intricate forms without breaking. The copper in the Arizona climate weathers to a deep bronze instead of the green patina that is seen in most of the United States.

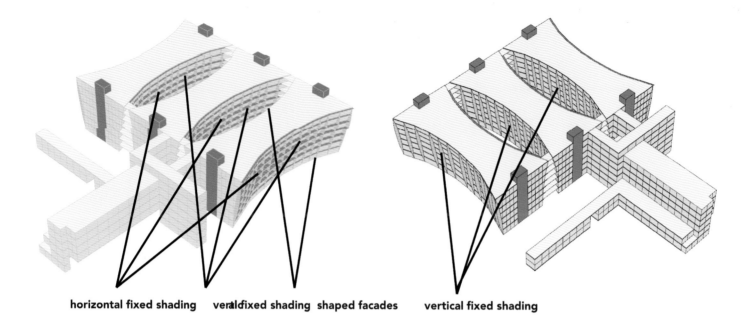

horizontal fixed shading   vertical fixed shading shaped facades   vertical fixed shading

[TOP] Early solar studies of the building.
[ABOVE] Detail of the folded copper panels before weathering.

The pattern of folds on the panels is a digitized abstraction based on photos of canyons and cactus. Working closely with a local copper fabricator, the design team figured out a way to create a system of standard panel types that could be combined to mimic the random patterns of nature.

The copper panels are part of a rainscreen system used in other buildings like the Barnes Foundation and the South Mountain Community Library. For the Health Sciences Education Building, CO Architects adapted the technology to form a sunscreen. Instead of directing rain away from the building, the screen system sheds heat before it penetrates the building.

CO Architects continued the sustainable design measures with simple siting and shading moves throughout the project. The designers oriented the building in an east-to-west direction to minimize the amount of direct sunlight the surfaces receive and to reduce heat gain. Deep overhangs and canopies provide shade on the south while vertical fins control low sun on the north. The bent angles of the building also help the building shade itself.

The Health Sciences Education Building is a thoughtful study of climate and a creative response to the nature of a place. Inspired by the project's environment, CO Architects created a building that supports the collaborative and interdisciplinary purpose of the Phoenix Biomedical Campus.

[FAR LEFT] CO Architects examine a full-size copper panel. Almost all of the quarter million pounds of copper in the skin is recycled.

[LEFT MIDDLE] Stephen with CO Architects in their office.

[LEFT] Detail of the copper rainscreen system showing how perforations allow light into the building.

[FAR LEFT] Aerial model of the site.
[LEFT] Sketch of an early plan study.

Yale Health Center

by Mack Scogin Merrill Elam Architects
New Haven, Connecticut

The new home of Yale University's Health Services is a cutting edge micro-hospital that reverses the traditional ideas of hospital design and planning. Mack Scogin Merrill Elam Architects won the project through a design competition for the site plan of a new building to replace the university's health services center. The firm's bold yet practical design impressed the selection committee, which included the dean of the Yale School of Architecture, Robert A.M. Stern, and former dean Cesar Pelli.

The program for the small site between a public park and a cemetery included a large amount of parking. The footprint required by the parking took up much of the space and left an irregularly shaped piece of land. Architects Mack Scogin and Merrill Elam accepted that following the strange geometry of the site to shape the footprint of the building would allow for the most square footage. Although each floorplate is basically a triangle, every building level grows and morphs from the previous one so that the structure expands as it moves upward. The architects then wrapped the resulting shape of the stacked floors and carved the wrapper into slightly convex and concave facades. The softly curved forms respond to the architecture of the University's Ingalls Rink and Stiles and Morse Colleges, by architect Eero Saarinen.

[ABOVE LEFT] The custom black brick alternates rows of flat and bull-nosed profiles.
[ABOVE] The upper floors of the building become progressively larger.
[FAR LEFT] View of the path cutting between the garage and the Health Center.
[LEFT] Mack offers details on the custom black brick.

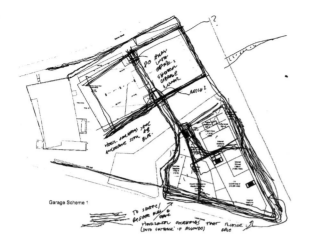

Garage Scheme 1

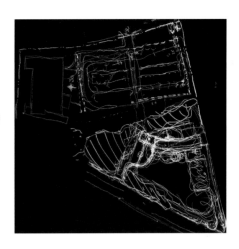

[LEFT] Sketch of the triangular site and parking garage.
[RIGHT] Sketch of an early plan study.
[BELOW] Concept model of the Yale Health Center showing the basic shape of the building.
[BELOW RIGHT] Figure ground study of the site and adjacent campus buildings.

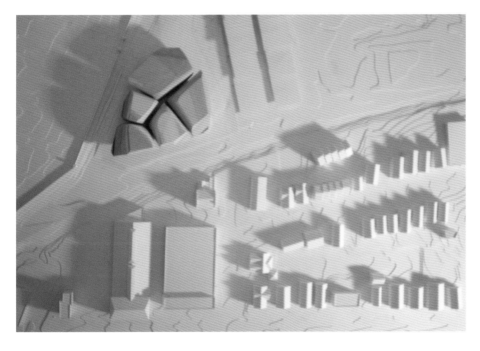

Yale University is a distinguished institution, and most of its buildings are appropriately dignified. Scogin and Elam wanted to give the Health Center a similarly substantial feel and chose a custom black brick for the skin. Although the clients were concerned about the image of a black building next to a cemetery, the architects believed that the building should be dark to complement the cemetery. They felt a light-colored building would be too stark against the dark stone walls surrounding the cemetery.

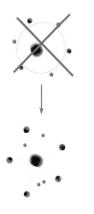

tentacular / radiating circulation

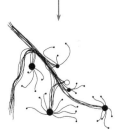

superimposed levels:
circulation and waiting nodes

circulation privacy progression

conceptual daylight diagram

[LEFT] Diagrams of the building's main concepts and organizing ideas.
[BELOW] View of the atrium ceiling showing overhead bridges.

The black bricks that clad the Health Center alternate between rounded, or bull-nosed, and flat profiles to create a large-scale pattern that can be read across the building. The individual bricks also express a human scale understandable from up close.

The very dark exterior contrasts with the bright interior spaces and flips the traditional idea of stark white hospitals with dark interiors. The architects wanted to create an uplifting environment that did not feel institutional. While the outside of the Yale Health Center projects a serious, strong image, the interior presents a peaceful, soft quality.

Hospitals are highly specialized building types that are usually designed by professional hospital planners. Scogin, however, rejected the typical ideas of hospital planning and developed an improved hospital experience from the patient's perspective. The architect inverted the traditional organization of a hospital, in which patients enter at the bright edges of the building and move toward dark centers. In the Yale Health Center, the entrance is at the center of the building in a four-story atrium. The atrium acts like a pinwheel by directing patients out to different departments through radiating

[LEFT] View of the central atrium with angled walls and jagged windows.

[RIGHT] View of the angled walls and windows which provide light and privacy in the atrium.

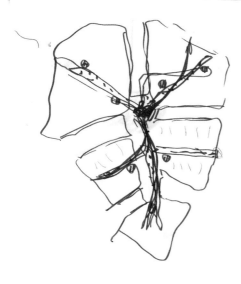

corridors. The design team used light to guide people through the building by placing the patient rooms and doctors' offices on the perimeter. As patients move from corridors to clinic reception areas and finally to exam and treatments rooms, the spaces become brighter and more private.

Protecting privacy and providing dignity were major concerns for the design team and the university. Because the health facility is used by a community of people who know each other, the architects made every effort to keep the sensitive activity of going to a doctor very private. Angled corridor walls and stairs shield views and special acoustics protect patient doctor privacy. Reception and waiting areas that look into the atrium are also angled so that patients can enjoy natural light but remain shielded. The atrium glass is frosted to allow light in but maintain privacy.

The Yale Health Center restructured the hospital experience for the students and health professionals of Yale University. Mack Scogin Merril Elam Architects broke down the institutional feel of a hospital to create a distinctive linchpin of the current and future campus.

[OPPOSITE TOP] Concept sketch of the building's circulation, guiding patients to more private but brighter spaces.
[RIGHT] Mack illustrates a design point for Stephen.
[BOTTOM RIGHT] Merrill and Mack in a brightly lit patient room.

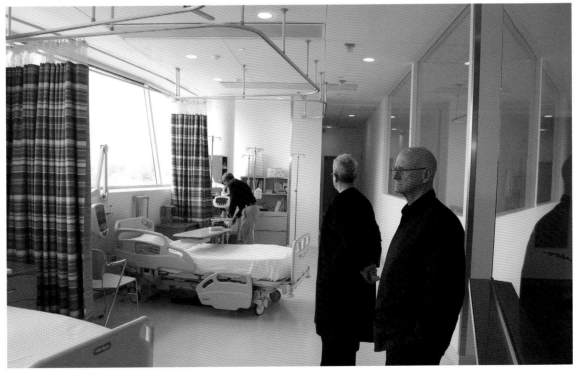

Credits

Bloch Building at the Nelson-Atkins Museum of Art

Images of sketches and models, courtesy and copyright Steven Holl Architects

Photos courtesy Nelson-Atkins Museum of Art, Steven Holl Architects

Photos copyright Andy Ryan, Roland Halbe, Kansas City Star, Timothy Hursley

Barnes Foundation

Images of sketches and models, courtesy and copyright Tod Williams Billie Tsien Architects

Photos courtesy Barnes Foundation, Tod Williams Billie Tsien Architects

Photos copyright Tom Crane, Dmadeo flickr, AngelaN flickr, Donnell flickr

Harvey B. Gantt Center for African-American Arts + Culture

Images of sketches and models, courtesy and copyright Freelon Group

Photos courtesy Harvey B. Gantt Center for African-American Arts + Culture, Freelon Group

Photos copyright Mark Herboth

Seattle Central Library

Images of sketches and models, courtesy and copyright OMA/REX

Photos courtesy OMA/REX

Photos copyright Iwan Baan, SanthoshRajangam flickr, Jvare flickr

James B. Hunt Jr. Library

Images of sketches and models, courtesy and copyright Snohetta

Photos courtesy Snohetta

Photos copyright Mark Herboth

South Mountain Community Library

Images of sketches and models, courtesy and copyright Richärd+Bauer

Photos courtesy Richärd+Bauer

Photos copyright Bill Timmerman, Mark Bosclair

Background information courtesy Arlen Solochek, Toni Garvey, Shera Farnham

Dallas Cowboys Stadium

Images of sketches and models, courtesy and copyright HKS Architects

Photos courtesy HKS Architects

Photos copyright HKS Architects, WKlos flickr, slgckgc flickr, mabecerra flickr, DavidJones flickr

Kauffman Center for the Performing Arts

Images of sketches and models, courtesy and copyright Moshe Safdie Architects

Photos courtesy Kauffman Center for the Performing Arts, Moshe Safdie Architects

Photos copyright Timothy Hursley, John Horner

Barclays Center

Images of sketches and models, courtesy and copyright SHoP Architects

Photos courtesy SHoP Architects

Photos copyright Bruce Damonte, Julie Jira

Lou Ruvo Center for Brain Health

Images of sketches and models, courtesy and copyright Gehry Partners

Photos courtesy Gehry Partners

Photos copyright Cygnusloop99, Whiting Turner

Health Sciences Education Building

Images of sketches and models, courtesy and copyright CO Architects

Photos courtesy CO Architects, Health Sciences Education Building

Photos copyright Bill Timmerman

Yale Health Center

Images of sketches and models, courtesy and copyright Mack Scogin Merrill Elam Architects

Photos courtesy Mack Scogin Merrill Elam Architects, Yale University

Photos copyright Timothy Hursley, Yale University Press

Acknowledgements

The Cool Spaces concept began as a television show and soon expanded to include a website and book. With so much work to do, it takes a team of talented professionals to make it all happen. We want to extend a special thank you to our team:

Rick Pack,
Branding/Sponsorships,
National Sponsorship Group

Braulio Agnese,
Managing Editor

Dan Frank,
Director/Producer,
Hawkes Media Group

John Hawkes,
Director of Photography,
Hawkes Media Group

Christie Boyle and Samantha Nestor,
Chrysanthemum Partners

Joseph Chung,
Graphics/Design

Alan Foster,
Executive Programs Services

Hope Reed,
Station Relations

Thank you to the television show underwriters for Season 1:

American Institute of Architects

Bluebeam

And thank you to our educational outreach partner:

Northeastern University School of Architecture

And a special thank you to Gordon Goff at ORO Editions for believing in this book project.

Index of Architecture Firms

STEVEN HOLL ARCHITECTS
450 West 31st Street, 11th floor
New York, NY 10001
1 212 629 7262
www.stevenholl.com

TOD WILLIAMS BILLIE TSIEN
ARCHITECTS
222 Central Park South
New York, NY 10019
1 212 582 2385
www.twta.com

THE FREELON GROUP
P.O. Box 12876
Research Triangle Park, NC 27709
1 919 941 9790
www.freelon.com

OFFICE FOR METROPOLITAN
ARCHITECTURE (OMA)
180 Varick Street, Suite 1328
New York, NY 10014
1 212 337 0770
www.oma.eu

REX
20 Jay Street Suite 920
Brooklyn, NY 11201 USA
1 646 230 6557
www.rex-ny.com

LMN ARCHITECTS
801 2nd Ave # 501
Seattle, WA 98104
1 206 682 3460
www.lmnarchitects.com

SNOHETTA
Akershusstranda 21
N-0150 Oslo, Norway
47 24 15 60 60
www.snohetta.com

CLARK NEXSEN
333 Fayetteville Street, Suite 1000
Raleigh, NC 27601
1 919 836 9751
www.clarknexsen.com

RICHARD + BAUER
1545 West Thomas Road
Phoenix, AZ 85015
1 602 264 1955
www.richard-bauer.com

HKS ARCHITECTS
350 N Saint Paul Street Suite 100
Dallas, TX 75201
1 214 969 5599
www.hksinc.com

MOSHE SAFDIE ARCHITECTS
100 Properzi Way
Somerville, MA 02143
1 617 629 2100
www.msafdie.com

SHoP ARCHITECTS
11 Park Pl #1909
New York, NY 10007
1 212 889 9005
www.shoparc.com

AECOM
100 Park Avenue
New York , NY 10017
1 212 973 2999
www.aecom.com

GEHRY PARTNERS
12541 Beatrice St.
Los Angeles, CA 90066
1 310 482 3000
www.foga.com

CO ARCHITECTS
5055 Wilshire Boulevard, 9th Floor
Los Angeles, CA 90036
1 323 525 0500
www.coarchitects.com

AYERS SAINT GROSS
60 E. Rio Salado Parkway, Suite 701
Tempe, AZ 85281
1 480 921 1515
www.asg-architects.com

MACK SCOGIN MERRILL ELAM
ARCHITECTS
111 John Wesley Dobbs Ave NE
Atlanta, GA 30303
1 404 525 6869
www.msmearch.com

Publishers of Architecture, Art, and Design
Gordon Goff: Publisher

www.oroeditions.com
info@oroeditions.com

USA, EUROPE, ASIA, MIDDLE EAST, SOUTH AMERICA

Published by ORO Editions

Graphic Design: Lynne Yeamans
Edited by: Sun Joo Kim and Ryan Buresh
Production Assistance: Alexandria Nazar
Text:
Project Coordinator: Sun Joo Kim

10 9 8 7 6 5 4 3 2 1 First Edition

Library of Congress data available upon request. World Rights: Available

ISBN: 978-1-941806-33-3

Color Separations and Printing: ORO Group Ltd.
Printed in China.

International Distribution: www.oroeditions.com/distribution